Two Lives of Saint Brigid

TWO LIVES OF
SAINT BRIGID

EDITED AND TRANSLATED BY

Philip Freeman

FOUR COURTS PRESS

Set in ACaslonPro 11.5pt/15.5pt by
Carrigboy Typesetting Services for
FOUR COURTS PRESS LTD
7 Malpas Street, Dublin 8, Ireland
www.fourcourtspress.ie
and in North America for
FOUR COURTS PRESS
c/o IPG, 814 N Franklin St, Chicago, IL 60610

A catalogue record for this title is available
from the British Library.

ISBN 978-1-80151-116-2

Printed in England by
CPI Antony Rowe, Chippenham, Wilts

CONTENTS

INTRODUCTION

We know almost nothing about the historical Saint Brigid aside from the fact that she was born in the middle of the fifth century in Ireland and founded a monastery for both men and men at Kildare on the plains of Leinster, west of Dublin. Brigid lived and worked at a time when Christianity was a relatively new and foreign religion in Ireland.

Like most early Christian hagiography, the life of Brigid is portrayed as a series of miracles recorded to prove her devotion to God. The accounts of her life provide a rich and informative picture of Irish culture and life at the time of their composition over a century after her death as well as the development of her cult, but they cannot be strictly relied on for biographical details of Brigid herself. Biography, however, was never the point of hagiography. The Brigid presented in her two earliest Latin *Lives* is a woman of the deepest faith and devotion to God. Her stories were recorded primarily to inspire Christians to a more holy life and should be read as such. Brigid's miracles were most often based on the Bible, especially the Gospels, as when Jesus turns water into wine at the wedding at Cana while Brigid turns water into beer. But in her miracles Brigid often manipulates nature and communicates with animals in a way uncommon in the Gospels, prompting many to suppose that the stories sometimes draw on pre-Christian Irish sources and traditions.

There was in fact a goddess named Brigid in Irish and wider Celtic religion before the arrival of Christianity. This goddess – whose name means 'the exalted one' – was actually a trinity of three goddesses associated with healing, poetry and ironworking. It was natural and advantageous for Christians establishing a new faith in Ireland to draw on the traditions and stories of native religion as much as possible to ease the transition of new converts. But whether or not such syncretism was deliberate, some aspects of the goddess Brigid are probably present in the stories of the saint. It can be no coincidence that the day of her death, thereafter celebrated as her feast day, is 1 February, the same day as the key pre-Christian festival of Imbolc marking the beginning of the Irish agricultural season with the birth of lambs. Even so, efforts to present St Brigid as a thinly-veiled pagan figure from an earlier time – a kind of baptized goddess – are well-meaning but misguided. The Brigid we have from her earliest stories and later traditions is an orthodox Christian devoted to good works as a means to serve God and spread the Gospel.

The stories of Brigid that were told since her own lifetime soon became part of Christian folklore, with her cult spreading in time beyond Ireland to Britain and continental Europe with the wanderings of Irish missionaries. She was embraced throughout Europe and especially in Ireland itself as 'the Mary of the Gaels' – a type of the Virgin Mary herself. For the last fifteen centuries she has been and remains an object of devotion to Christians in Ireland and chief among female saints.

The two earliest Latin *Lives* of Brigid which are the subject of this book are the *Life of Saint Brigid* by Cogitosus and the anonymous *Vita Prima*. We know nothing for certain about the writer of the *Vita Prima* and very little about Cogitosus. Muirchú, the author of the earliest Life of Patrick in the late seventh century, calls Cogitosus his father, but this is almost certainly meant in a spiritual and literary rather than biological sense. This would place Cogitosus in the mid-seventh century, perhaps a hundred years after the death of Brigid. His writing shows a strong bias towards the primacy of the church at Kildare as opposed to the rival ecclesiastical seat at Armagh in the north of Ireland, so it is reasonable to assume Cogitosus was associated with the monastery Brigid founded. Armagh was the centre of the competing cult of Patrick by this time, so he is conspicuous in never mentioning the more famous saint. He also is insistent that Kildare is the head of all the Irish churches, showing that ecclesiastical politics are alive and well in his *Life*. For sources, Cogitosus claims he drew on stories of Brigid handed down to him by his elders. As for language and style, his Latin is quite polished, with enough classical and Christian literary allusions and references to show a solid education and deep familiarity with the broader hagiographical tradition.

The anonymous *Vita Prima* is so named because it was placed before Cogitosus in the *Acta Sanctorum*, a collection of the Lives of the saints done in 1658 by the religious society of the Bollandists, known for their hagiographical work.[1] The *Vita Prima* is more than twice the length of Cogitosus' *Life*, with over thirty of the same miracle episodes included though presented in differing ways. The Latin of the author, while still quite good, is not as polished as that of Cogitosus. Aside from length, the primary difference between the two *Lives* is that in the *Vita Prima* Brigid frequently travels across all the provinces of Ireland, with Kildare mentioned only once, giving it the sense of a national rather than local narrative. Cogitosus, on the other hand, has Brigid leave the area of Kildare only once and then she does not travel far. Another notable difference is that Brigid in the *Vita Prima* meets St Patrick a number of times and is clearly portrayed as subordinate to him. There are no claims of national ecclesiastical authority for Brigid in the *Vita Prima*, arguing for an author with a political agenda supporting Kildare's rival church in Armagh. This is not at all to say the Brigid of the *Vita Prima* is a meek or uninteresting figure. If anything she is a more forceful and uncompromising character than in Cogitosus' *Life*, but one who bends the knee to Patrick as her superior.

There is a third early Life story of Brigid not included in this volume but that should be mentioned. This text is called the *Bethu Brigte* and was composed mainly in Old Irish with about one quarter in Latin. The *Bethu Brigte* is preserved only in one medieval

1   *The Life of Saint Brigid* by Cogitosus was listed second in the *Acta Sanctorum*, giving it the title *Vita Secunda* or *Vita II* by which it is still sometimes known.

manuscript and has been admirably edited and translated by Donncha Ó hAodha.[2] It is missing the very beginning of Brigid's life due to the loss of a manuscript leaf and is even shorter in total length than Cogitosus' *Life*. The brief collection of miracle stories in the *Bethu Brigte* are closely related to the *Vita Prima* and share a substantial amount of the same material.

There has long been a controversy as to the relationship between and relative chronology of these three earliest *Lives* of Brigid.[3] The current consensus, though not unanimous, is that Cogitosus composed his *Life* before the other two sometime in the mid-seventh century based on earlier sources which have not survived. The *Vita Prima*, composed later, may well have used Cogitosus as a source, but also draws on other traditions. The *Bethu Brigte*, while closely related to the *Vita Prima*, seems not to derive from it but uses at least some of the same source material.

The value and usefulness of the *Life of Saint Brigid* of Cogitosus and the *Vita Prima* have long suffered from the lack of proper Latin editions and the scattered nature of the English translations. Both works were first edited from limited and often inferior Latin manuscripts in the previously mentioned *Acta Sanctorum* of the mid-seventeenth century, but there has been no complete Latin edition published of either *Life* since then.[4] There have however been two excellent English translations of both works that are more widely available.[5] But there has never been a translation of both

2 Ó hAodha, *Bethu Brigte* (1978).
3 For a history and discussion of this debate, see Ó hAodha, *Bethu Brigte*, xvii–xxvii; Kim McCone, 'Brigit in the seventh century: a saint with three Lives?', *Peritia* 1 (1982), 107–45; Richard Sharpe, '*Vitae S Brigitae*: the oldest texts', *Peritia* 1 (1982), 81–106.
4 In 1970, Seán Connolly wrote for his dissertation at the National University of Ireland a critical Latin edition of the *Vita Prima* – '*Vita Prima Sanctae Brigitae*: a critical edition with introduction, commentary and indices' (PhD, NUI, 1970) – but this unfortunately has remained unpublished and difficult to access. I myself published a preliminary Latin edition of Cogitosus's *Life* in the *Proceedings of the Harvard Celtic Colloquium* 39 (2019), 109–33.
5 S. Connolly, '*Vita Prima Sanctae Brigitae*: background and historical value', *The Journal of the Royal Society of Antiquaries of Ireland* 119 (1989), 5–49; S. Connolly,

Lives in one volume. This book presents original English translations as well as the edited Latin texts of Cogitosus' *Life* and the *Vita Prima*.

My modest goal in this volume is to offer for the first time translations of both *Lives* along with the Latin texts for interested readers, students and scholars, with the hope that it will provide a resource for further research and study.[6] I have resisted the scholarly urge to overburden the text with notes and commentary, limiting these primarily to biblical references.

Compared to many medieval Latin works, we have an abundance of surviving manuscripts of both of the early Latin *Lives* of Brigid. This is a testimony to the popularity of the saint among readers of the era. Interestingly, none of the earliest manuscripts are from Ireland but rather from Britain or the European continent where the stories were originally taken by travelling Irish monks. I have worked with librarians in these countries to locate, access and in some cases commission for the first time high-quality images of the most important sources of both *Lives* for use in this volume.

There are over eighty surviving manuscripts of the *Life of Saint Brigid* by Cogitosus dating from the ninth to seventeenth centuries.[7] The earliest and best manuscripts are:

R –   Reims, Bibliothèque de la Ville 296 (9th/10th century) From the nearby Benedictine abbey of Saint-Thierry, the Cogitosus material is found on folios 101r–113r and is complete.

B –   Berlin, Staatsbibliothek 364 (10th century) Originally from the Benedictine monastery of Saint Liudgerus at Werden in

and J.-M. Picard, 'Cogitosus' *Life of St Brigit*: content and value', *The Journal of the Royal Society of Antiquaries of Ireland* 117 (1987), 5–27.

6   Many excellent studies of the content of the two Lives have been published, including those listed in the Bibliography.

7   Ludwig Bieler lists these in the *Manuscript sources for the history of Irish civilisation* (1965), 332–4. Bieler offers only the briefest description of each of these manuscripts, but more detailed studies of many of the manuscripts are available in M. Esposito, 'On the earliest Latin Life of St Brigid of Kildare', *PRIA* C 30.11 (1912/13), 307–19, and Esposito, 'Cogitosus', *Hermathena* 20 (1926), 251–7.

western Germany, the manuscript is complete on folios 73r–85r except for the omission of the prologue.

Br – Brussels, Bibliothèque Royale II.2568 (10th century) From the abbey of Stavelot in eastern Belgium, the Cogitosus material is complete on folios 48v–59r aside from the omission of the prologue.

O – Orleans, Bibliothèque Publique 311 (10th century) From the Benedictine monastery at Fleury, south of Paris or the nearby monastery at Saint-Benoît-sur-Loire, complete on pages 266–78.

P_I – Paris, Bibliothèque Nationale Latin 10862 (10th century) From the Benedictine abbey at Echternach in Luxembourg, complete on folios 1r–24r

C – Cambrai, Bibliothèque Municipale 865 (10th/11th century) Formerly at the Cathedral Library at Cambrai in northern France, complete on folios 115v–123v.

L – London, British Library Cotton Nero E1 (11th century) Written in England on folios 134v–140r with a missing section, this manuscript also contains some of the earliest copies of the two letters of St Patrick. It is closely related to Salisbury manuscript 221 below.

Bg – Bergamo 227 (11th century) Complete on folios 60r–67r, the manuscript is from the Biblioteca del Clero di S. Alessandro in Colonna at Bergamo in northern Italy.

M – Munich 18854 (11th century) Formerly at the Benedictine monastery of Tegernsee in Bavaria, complete on folios 85r–112r.

N – Naples VIII.B.3 (11th century) Provenance unknown, complete on folios 379r–388v.

P_2 – Paris, Bibliothèque Mazarine 1711 (11th century) From a large volume of the lives of the saints, complete on folios 237v–247v.

P_3 – Paris, Bibliothèque Nationale Latin 2999 (11th century) From the Benedictine monastery of Saint-Amand in northern France, the Cogitosus material begins on 36r but is incomplete.

Rn – Rouen, Bibliothèque Municipale MS 1384 (11th century) From the Benedictine abbey of Jumièges near Rouen in northern France, complete on folios 230v–240v.

S – Salisbury 221 (11th/12th century) Previously in the Bodleian Library listed as Oxford Fell 4, the Cogitosus material on folios 108r–116v has the same gap as the London manuscript above.

The oldest and most reliable manuscript of Cogitosus' work is from the Bibliothèque de la Ville at Reims in northeast France, originally housed at the nearby Benedictine abbey of Saint-Thierry. This witness to Cogitosus has formed the basis of my edition with only minor changes in those cases when another manuscript offers a better reading.

There are just over thirty manuscripts of the *Vita Prima* which survive from the ninth to the seventeenth centuries.[8] Most of the later manuscripts add little to our understanding of the text, but the five earliest versions are important for reconstructing the original text. These are:

L – London, British Library Additional Manuscript 34124 (9th century) Originating in Bavaria and probably written by a German scribe, the *Vita Prima* makes up the entire manuscript (124 folios) and is complete.

P – Paris, Bibliothèque Nationale Latin 10864 (10th century) Formerly belonging to the Benedictine monastery of Echternach in Luxembourg, the *Vita Prima* is found on folios 99r–123v and is incomplete.

8 Bieler (1965), 331–2. More detailed discussion of many of the manuscripts are found in M. Esposito, 'On the earliest Latin Lives of St Brigid of Kildare', *Hermathena* (1935), 140–4, and Connolly, 'The authorship and manuscript tradition of *Vita I Sanctae Brigitae*', *Manuscripta* 16 (1972), 67–82.

M – Munich, Bayerische Staatsbibliothek Clm 2531 (10th century) A collection of the lives of women saints from the monastery of Aldersbach in Bavaria, the text on folios 128v–192v is incomplete.

Z – Zurich, Zentralbibliothek Rheinau 81 (10th/11th century) Paginated with the *Vita Prima* on pages 4–89, the manuscript is incomplete.

H – Heiligenkreuz Zisterzienserstift 11 (12th century) Found in a collection of lives of the saints from the Cistercian monastery of Heilingenkreuz in Austria, the text is complete on folios 96v–105v.

As with the *Life of St Brigid* by Cogitosus, a single manuscript stands as both the earliest and best reflection of the original text of the *Vita Prima*, the one now found in London's British Library. I have used this manuscript as the base text of my Latin edition, amending it only when the reading is obviously wrong or is better attested by one of the other early witnesses, usually the Paris manuscript. I have also maintained the forms and variations found in the London manuscript (e.g. *-e* for *-ae*, *Brigita* usually instead of *Brigida*). An exception to this is the spelling of Irish names in the text, for which I have preferred the Paris manuscript as it almost always records the original forms better than the other witnesses.

The base texts of the manuscripts – Reims (R) for Cogitosus and London (L) for the *Vita Prima* – are used in my edition except when noted. The variants are listed by manuscript abbreviations (e.g. B for Berlin, H for Heiligenkreuz) and given only when an alternate reading is better or of particular interest. On a very few occasions I have made an unattested emendation when I felt the Latin text is clearly wrong, but have listed any manuscript attestations of that reading for comparison.

Finally, in my translations I have tried to be as literal as good English allows, preserving when possible the style and rhythm of the medieval authors to give readers a sense of the Latin originals.

The Life of Saint Brigid by Cogitosus

THE LIFE OF SAINT BRIGID

Here begins the life of holy Brigid the virgin whose feast day is the first of February.

PROLOGUE

Brothers, you compel me to undertake to record in writing for posterity, in the way of learned men, the miracles and works of the virgin Brigid of holy and blessed memory. This task imposed on me is difficult because of its delicate subject matter and because I am woefully ignorant and have no skill with language. But God is powerful enough to make great things from the least, just as he did when he filled the house of the poor widow from a small amount of oil and a handful of grain.[1]

And so compelled by your commands, I have not been lacking in my obedience. I have therefore made known a few of the many stories handed down by well-informed elders. I present these plainly and without any shadow of ambiguity lest I incur the charge of disobedience.

Through these stories I hope that this virgin of greatness and worth abounding in glorious virtues becomes known in the eyes of everyone. Not that my memory and mediocrity and rustic speech or my limited ability could be adequate to accomplish the duty of such a great task. But by your blessed faith and daily prayers I hope to merit success beyond the ability of this narrator.

Thus she – growing in extraordinary virtues and in reputation of good works with countless people of both sexes coming to her from all the provinces of the whole of Ireland and freely making their vows to her – built her own monastery as the head of almost all the

---

1 1 Kings 17:8–16. In the story the prophet Elijah miraculously makes the small portion of oil and grain belonging to a widow last for many days.

churches of the Irish and as the summit surpassing all the monasteries of the Irish, whose *parochia* is spread through all the land of the Irish and extends from sea to sea.[2] She built her monastery in the broad plain of the Liffey on the firm foundation of faith.[3]

And taking care of the souls of her people by prudent administration in all things according to rules and being greatly concerned for her followers in the churches in all the provinces, she realized that she could not be without a high priest who could consecrate churches and confer holy orders in them. She therefore sent for a renowned man and solitary, Conleth, known for all his good qualities, through whom God had worked many miracles. She called him from the wilderness and his solitary life and set out to meet him, so that he might govern the church in episcopal dignity with her and so that nothing regarding priestly offices would be lacking in her churches.

And thus afterwards the anointed head and leader of all the bishops along with the most blessed chief of nuns, in happy partnership and guided by all virtues, ruled together their principal church. By the merits of both their episcopal and feminine authority, it grew like a fruitful vine with spreading branches throughout the whole island of Ireland. Her church has continued to be ruled in happy succession and perpetual rite by the archbishop of the Irish bishops and the abbess whom all the abbesses of the Irish revere.

Thus, as I said above, compelled by the brothers, I will try to relate, with great concern for brevity, the miracles performed by this blessed Brigid, both those miracles done before she became an abbess and those others done after, with the former first.

Thus ends the preface concerning the miracles of holy Brigid.

2 Latin *par(r)ochia* or *paruchia*, an area of ecclesiastical jurisdiction or influence.
3 At Kildare, west of modern Dublin, near the Liffey River.

1. And so holy Brigid, whom God foreknew and predestined to his image,[4] was born to Christian and noble parents from the good and most wise clan of Echtech in Ireland, born of her father Dubthach and her mother Broicsech. From her childhood she grew in her desire of good things. Indeed this girl chosen by God and self-restrained in behaviour for her age and full of modesty, was always ripening into better things.

But who could possibly tell all of her works and miracles she did even at that age? I will only relate these few of the countless deeds she performed as an example.

When she was old enough, she was sent by her mother to the task of churning so that she could turn into butter the stirred cow's milk. Just as other women were accustomed to do this work, she also did so in the same manner. And with the others at the assigned time she was to return for use the yield of the cows and the accustomed weight and measure of butter in full.

But this virgin, most beautiful in her ways and kindness, wishing to obey God more than people, gave away freely to the poor and guests the milk and butter.

And when as usual the appointed time came for everyone to hand over the yield of the cows, her turn came. And after her co-workers had given over their finished work, it was required from the previously mentioned blessed maiden that she in the same way hand over her work.

And she was in dreadful fear of her mother's anger since she did not have anything to show, having given away everything to the poor, not thinking of the future. But burning with the unquenchable fire of faith and firm, she prayed as she turned herself to the Lord.

Without delay the Lord, hearing the voice of the virgin and her prayers, with generosity of the divine gift, for he is a helper in hours of need, was present. And for her sake since the virgin was trusting in him, he generously restored the butter.

4   Rom 8:29.

Marvellous it was that in that hour after her prayer the most holy virgin showed that there was nothing lacking from her work, but more abundantly than her co-workers she proved that she had done her duty.

And when the miracle of such a great gift was fully known in the eyes of everyone, they praised God who had done such a deed and marvelled at the power of faith that dwelled in the heart of the virgin.

2. It was not long after this when her parents, as is the custom, wished to promise her in marriage to a man. But she, inspired by heaven and wishing instead to offer herself to God as a chaste virgin, went to the most holy Bishop Mac Caille of blessed memory. He was impressed by the heavenly longing and modesty and great love of chastity in that virgin and so he placed a white veil and a shining garment over her venerable head.

Before God and the bishop, she fell humbly to her knees in front of the altar and offered her virginal crown to the Lord almighty, touching the wood at the base of the altar with her hand.

That wood, because of the purity of her virtue, even to the present time is green as if it had not been cut and stripped of its bark but is still attached to its roots. Even to this day it drives away sickness and disease from all the faithful.

3. I should not omit recording the story of another miracle which that most famous handmaid of God performed, who was ceaselessly devoted to divine service.

Once when she had cooked bacon in a cauldron for guests who were arriving, she gave some of it in compassion to a fawning and begging dog.

And when the bacon was taken from the cauldron and after-wards divided among the guests, it was found completely intact as if none had been taken away.

And indeed those who saw this, admiring the young woman incomparable in the virtue of faith and in the merit of her good virtues, spread the story with worthy praise.

4. Once she called together reapers and workers to her harvest. And when the gathering of harvesters occurred, the day of the gathering was cloudy and wet with abundant rain pouring from the clouds all around that whole province. Streams of gushing water overflowed the glens and gullies of the land, with only her harvest remaining dry without a hindrance or damage from the rain.[5]

And although all the harvesters of that surrounding region were prevented from working that day, her workers laboured in their task without a shadow of a rain cloud that whole day from the rising to the setting of the sun by the power of God.

5. Indeed, among the other miracles of this woman, this deed seems to be admirable.

Once when bishops were coming and staying with her, although she did not have anything to feed them, her needs were provided abundantly by the manifold power of God, as was usual.

She milked one and the same cow three times on a single day, contrary to normal. And what was accustomed to be produced from three of the best cows, she milked from her one cow, amazing to be told.

6. Also this miracle, you blessed ones, I must include, in which the pure virginal mind and the helping divine hand appear to come together in one accord.

For after she was tending her sheep in her pastoral work on a flat and grassy place, she was soaked by a fierce downpour of rain and she went into a house in wet clothes.

And with a ray of the sun coming into the house through an opening, she, with her eyes dazzled and thinking it to be a slanted

---

5 An inversion of a more common miracle (e.g. 1 Kings 18:41–6) in the desert setting of the Bible in which a lack of rain is relieved through divine intervention.

tree fixed there, putting her wet cloak on it, hung the cloak there on that insubstantial sunbeam as if it were a large and solid tree.

And the inhabitants of that house and the neighbours, struck as they were by this great miracle, extolled this extraordinary woman with worthy praise.

7. The following deed must also not be passed over in silence.

Once when holy Brigid was in a field tending and feeding her flock of sheep, diligent in her pastoral duties, a young scoundrel came to her cunningly and tested her generosity to the poor. Disguised in different clothes each time, he came to her seven times and received from her in one day seven sheep which he hid away in secret.

And when the flock in the evening, as was usual, was driven to the fold, they were carefully counted two or three times and miraculously found to be no less in number than when they were counted that morning.

And the companions who had helped steal the sheep, being astonished by the miracle of God done through the virgin, returned the seven stolen sheep to her flock.[6] But even then the count of the flock was found to be neither more nor less than it had been before.

Because of these and countless other miracles, this handmaid of very great fame was in the mouth of all, not undeservedly, but seemed most excellent and worthy of praise above all.

8. Here is another miraculous event about lepers seeking beer from venerable Brigid.[7] Although she had no beer, seeing water prepared for baths, she blessed it with the power of faith and turned it into the finest beer, then drew it out abundantly for the thirsty men.

So he who turned water into wine in Cana of Galilee also, through the faith of this most blessed woman, changed water into beer.[8]

---

6   Brigid's pardoning of the thief echoes the Gospel command to forgive offenders seven times (Mt 18:21–2; Lk 17:4).

7   Leprosy is found frequently in the Bible and was cured by Jesus on more than one occasion (e.g. Lk 17:11–19).

8   Jesus turned water into wine at the Cana wedding, his first miracle (Jn 2:1–11).

But having spoken of this miracle, it seems appropriate to make mention of another admirable deed.

9. By the most powerful and ineffable strength of faith, she blessed a certain woman who, after making a vow of chastity, had lapsed because of human frailty and youthful desire and became pregnant with a swelling womb. And when that which was conceived in her womb vanished, she restored the woman without childbirth and without pain in good health to repentence.

And in accord with the saying that all things are possible to those who believe,[9] she worked countless miracles every day without anything being impossible.

10. Again one day when a certain man came to her seeking salt, just as other poor and countless destitute people were accustomed to come to her about their needs, most blessed Brigid in that hour gave to the man seeking it an abundance of salt made from a stone which she had blessed.[10]

And thus carrying the salt from her, the happy man returned home.

11. And it seems to me that this most potent divine work of hers should be included among the others, by which, like the Saviour, as an imitator of the divine power she performed a truly extraordinary miracle. For following the example of the Lord, she also opened the eyes of one man born blind.[11] For the Lord has generously given his powers and abilities to his followers.

Although he says of himself, 'I am the light of the world',[12] nonetheless he also says to his disciples, 'You are the light of the world'.[13] And about them he also says, 'The works that I do, they will do also and greater than these they will do'.[14]

9 Mt 17:20; Mk 9:23.
10 Salt in the New Testament is a symbol of goodness and divine grace (e.g. Mt 5:13) and is used as such frequently in both Cogitosus' *Life* and the *Vita Prima*.
11 Jn 9:1–41. 12 Jn 8:12, 9:5. 13 Mt 5:14. 14 Jn 14:12.

Thus the one natural birth had brought forth blind from the womb, the faith of this Brigid, like a mustard seed,[15] opened to pure and shining vision by this great miracle.

12. Thus famous for such great miracles and filled with humility of heart and purity of mind and modesty of character and with spiritual grace, she was worthy to gain such authority in divine worship and a prestigious name above all the virgins of her time.

And on a certain day a woman follower of hers from outside the community came to her with her twelve-year-old daughter, mute from birth. With great reverence the mother bowed to her, as everyone did, and with her head lowered approached to receive a kiss of peace.

As Brigid was friendly and cheerful to all, she conversed with the woman warmly, sprinkling her words with divine salt. Then in the manner of our Saviour who ordered the little ones come to him,[16] she took the hand of the young girl in her own, not knowing she was mute, and asked her what her desire was, whether she wished to have her head veiled and be a virgin always or to be given in marriage.

When the mother warned that her daughter was not able to give a response, Brigid said she would not let go of the girl's hand until she herself answered. And when she asked the girl the same thing a second time, the girl answered her saying, 'I want to do nothing except what you want'.

And after that, with her mouth opened and without impediment to her tongue and her restraint removed, the healed girl was able to speak.

13. And who would not be moved by this deed of hers not heard before by the ears of many?

Once when she was intent in her spirit on her meditation of higher things, as was her custom, turning her thoughts from the

15 Mt 13:31–2.   16 Mt 19:14; Mk 10:14; Lk 18:16.

things of this earth to heavenly matters, she sent a piece of bacon –
a large piece, not at all small – away with a dog. And when the
bacon was sought, it was found exactly where the dog was
accustomed to stay. A month had passed, but they found the bacon
whole and untouched.

For the dog had not dared to eat something entrusted to him by
the blessed virgin, but had been a patient and proper guardian of
the bacon, contrary to his own nature. He proved himself tame and
restrained by a divine miracle.

14. And with the number of her miracles growing daily, which are
scarcely able to be counted, she was full of compassion and piety,
giving alms to the poor who asked whether it was convenient for
her or not.

When one needy person among the poor asked her for food, she
hurried to those cooking meat so that she might take some from
them to the poor person. But one very foolish servant among those
who were cooking meat stupidly placed a part of the meat not yet
completely cooked into the fold of her white mantle for her to hold.
And so she carried it back to the beggar with her mantle not only
unstained but keeping its shining white colour.

15. This wonder from her kindly works also ought to be admired.

With many poor people and pilgrims flocking to her from
everywhere, drawn by the great fame of her miracles and abundant
charity, there came among them a certain ungrateful leper who
demanded to be given the best cow of the herd together with the
best calf of all the calves.

Hearing this request she did not turn him away, but knowing the
cow that was the best of all and also knowing a beautiful calf of
another cow, she freely gave them both to the man who was asking
for them.

She even sent her own chariot with him for the journey over the
long and wide plain lest while driving the cow the sick man be

wearied by the long journey. She also ordered that the calf be placed behind him in the chariot.

And so the cow licked the calf with her tongue, caring for it as if it were her own with no one urging her and followed behind the chariot until they reached their destination.

So you see, my dearest brothers, that even brute animals served her contrary to their own nature.

16. After some time had passed, some most wicked thieves who feared neither God nor men came from another province on a raid. And easily crossing a wide river at a ford, they stole the cattle of Brigid.

But returning the same way, the force of the river, swollen greatly from a sudden rain, ruined their plans, for the river rising like a wall did not permit the most wicked thieves of blessed Brigid's cattle to pass over. It overwhelmed the thieves and dragged them away. The cattle were freed from their hands and with their leather ropes hanging from their horns, they returned to their herd and pen.

17. In this story divine power is also made clear.

When on a certain day the most holy Brigid, learning of some pressing need, set out to visit an assembly of the people sitting in a chariot drawn by two horses. And while in the vehicle in contemplative meditation bringing down the heavenly life from on high to earth, as was her custom, she prayed to the Lord.

But one of the horses, recklessly leaping under the chariot and twisting itself loose from its reins with force and slipping itself free of its yoke, ran terrified across the plain, while the other horse remained alone under its yoke.

And then the divine hand held up the yoke and kept it from falling while the crowd watched this testimony of divine power. With her praying peacefully in the chariot with a single horse in place, she arrived safely at the assembly of the people after a pleasant ride. Thus by signs and miracles confirming her teaching, she addressed the people with helpful words sprinkled with divine salt.

18. And it seems to us this should also be included among her miracles.

Once a single wild boar of the forest fled terrified in a mad rush into a herd of pigs of the most blessed Brigid. When she happened to see him among her pigs, she blessed him. Then he, unafraid and submissive, remained with her herd of pigs.

So you see, brothers, that even brute animals and beasts were not able to resist her words and wishes, but served her tamely and were subject to her will.

19. Once there was a certain man who came among others offering gifts to her. Arriving from a distant province, he offered her fat pigs and asked that she send some men with him to his farm located a long distance away so that they might collect the pigs from him. And so she sent her men with him for the long journey across the countryside of more than three or four days.

After a journey of a single day along a mountain bordering this region, the proper name of which is Gabor, they saw the man's own pigs which they had thought were far away, being directed and driven forward by wolves along the road.

And when the man understood they were his, realizing they were his own, and saw the wild wolves – who on account of great reverence for blessed Brigid, having come from vast forests and the very broad plain of the Liffey were labouring with great care as shepherds herding and driving the pigs – these wolves left the pigs unharmed when the men arrived, acting in a miraculous way and with great intelligence contrary to their nature.

And thus on the next day the men who had been sent returned home with the pigs, telling of the wondrous deed.

20. Again it seems to us that this deed from among her miraculous deeds must certainly not be passed over untold.

One day when a certain man lacking knowledge saw a fox walking through the settlement of a king, he thought it was a wild animal because his senses were blinded. He didn't know that it was in fact a tame and familiar animal in the court and was trained to do many tricks with great agility and cleverness for the king and his companions. And so in the sight of everyone, he killed it.

And then having been bound and denounced by those who saw him, the offender was led to the king. And the king was furious hearing what had happened and ordered him to be killed unless another similar fox was given to him which was able to do all the tricks of the previous animal. He would also take all his possessions and seize the wife and sons of the man and turn them into slaves.

When holy and venerable Brigid learned what had happened, she was moved greatly with pity and holy compassion. She ordered that her chariot be yoked, grieving in her inmost heart for that unfortunate man who had been unjustly judged. Pouring forth prayers to the Lord, she drove across the wide plain on the road which led to the king's settlement.

Without delay the Lord, hearing the ceaseless prayers she poured forth, sent one of his own wild foxes to her. The animal came bounding across the plain and jumped into most blessed Brigid's chariot. Hiding itself under her cloak, it rode tamely along with her in the chariot.

When Brigid came to the king, she began to beseech him to release the poor, ignorant fellow who was being held and to free him from his chains. And when the king would not listen to her prayers, insisting that he would not free the man unless he received another fox as tame and talented as the one he had before, then before the king and the multitude she produced the fox hiding under her cloak. This fox performed all the tricks of his predecessor with the docile subtlety and skill of the previous fox.

When the king saw this, he was satisfied and all his nobles burst into loud applause with the crowd admiring his tricks. The king ordered that the chains of the condemned man be removed and that he be set free.

Not long after this, holy Brigid, having secured the man's freedom and liberty, set off again to her home. But the cunning fox that looked like the other one, dashing quickly through the crowd and weaving in and out between the onlookers, ran away into the wild deserted places and forests to his den and escaped unharmed, outwitting the crowd of horsemen and hounds chasing it across the open plains.

And everyone, admiring this thing that had happened, venerated holy Brigid who was capable of performing always greater wonders because of the privilege of her holiness and her multitude of virtues.

21. When on another day blessed Brigid, seeing ducks swimming in the water as was their nature and flying here and there through the air, called to them to come to her. Flying on their wings with great eagerness to obey her calls as though they were accustomed to human care without any fear, the flocks came to her.

Touching them with her hand and embracing them and doing this for some time, she then allowed them to return, flying through the air on their wings. Praising the invisible creator of all things – to whom all living things are subject and by whom everything lives – through visible creatures,[17] as it says in the reciting of the holy service.

And from all these deeds clearly it can be understood that all of nature – beasts and cattle and birds – were subject to her will.

22. The following miracle of hers must be repeated to the ears of the faithful to be celebrated for all ages.

For when Brigid was sowing the most life-giving seeds of the Lord's word among all, as was her usual way, she saw nine men dressed in a certain form of their particular foolish and diabolical superstition. They were making a ridiculous noise and had

17 Col 1:16.

the greatest madness of mind. Their power was grief and unhappiness, the way of the ancient enemy who ruled over them. With most wicked vows and oaths, they were thirsting for blood and had sworn that before the beginning of that next month they would carry out a slaughter and murder of others.

The most reverent and kindly Brigid beseeched them with many calming words that they renounce the deadly error of their ways and erase their crimes through a piercing of their hearts and true repentance. But because of the dullness of their mind, they would not do this until they had fulfilled the vows they had made. And so they went on their way. But for this intention, pouring out prayers earnestly to the Lord, the renowned virgin, after the Lord's example, wished that all people would be saved and come to the knowledge of the truth.

And so when the evil men left her, they saw the image of the man they planned to kill and stabbed him repeatedly with their spears and cut off his head with their swords. Afterwards, as if in a triumphal parade over an adversary and enemy, marching back they appeared to many with weapons covered in blood and gore.

But the amazing thing is that they had killed no one at all, although it seemed to them they had fulfilled their vows. And since there was nobody missing from that province over whom they might have triumphed, and there was no doubt remaining concerning this matter, the generosity of this divine gift done through holy Brigid became known to all. And thus those men, who had been murderers before, were turned through repentance to the Lord.

23. And in this deed the divine power was made manifest through celebrated Brigid in a remarkable act of sacred faith.

Once there was a man named Lugaid who was a strong man and indeed the strongest of men. He was so powerful in his body that he could do the work of twelve men in one day when he wished, but he had such a large appetite that he also ate as much as twelve men.

Just as he alone could do their work, he was able to equal them by himself in eating as well.

He therefore asked Brigid if she would pray to the almighty Lord for him to help him temper his appetite which made him devour so much, but also not to lose the strength of body he had before.

And thus for this cause Brigid blessing him and praying to the Lord for him, he afterward was content with the food of a single man. And as he was accustomed before, he worked labouring like twelve men, so that he retained the same strength as earlier.

24. Again among her famous deeds, this outstanding and excellent work known to all I must discuss.

There was a certain tree, grand and magnificent, prepared for some use and cut down by those who were accustomed to such work with axes in a timber forest. A group of strong men gathered around the tree – which was awkward and huge and in a difficult location where it had fallen with a crash of its branches – to take it down and drag it away with many oxen and much lumbering equipment to the place where it was needed.

And when neither the multitude of men nor the strength of the oxen and various equipment of the workers were able to move or drag that tree in any way, they all withdrew from it. But through the very strong faith of blessed Brigid – which was like the grain of a mustard seed, a faith through which the Master of heaven, by means of the word of the Gospel, teaches us that mountains are moved,[18] just as all things are possible to those believing – they were allowed to carry this heaviest of trees without any difficulty by the strength of angels through divine assistance with no mortal help to the destination holy Brigid wanted.

And throughout all the provinces, news of this outstanding divine miracle was spread.

18 Mt 17:20–1.

25. And it seems to our mind impossible to exclude this miracle by our silence, which is among the many other miracles venerable Brigid performed.

Once there was a certain layman of both noble birth and wicked character who was burning with lust for a woman and cunningly plotting how he might have sex with her. And so he entrusted to her care his own silver brooch, which he then craftily stole back without her knowing and threw into the sea, so that when she would not be able to return it to him she would be his slave and afterwards he could use her sinfully as he wished.

He plotted to carry out this evil deed and declared that he would be able to be placated by no other thing except the return of his silver brooch or the woman becoming his slave to use to satisfy his most disgraceful desires.

And fearing these things, the chaste maiden fled to holy Brigid as to the safest city of refuge.[19] When Brigid heard her story, she was considering what to do for her when, even before she finished speaking, a certain man came to her with fish taken from the river. And when the insides of the fish had been cut open, that same silver brooch that the evil man had thrown into the sea for the reason mentioned above was discovered in the middle of one of the fish.[20]

And thus afterwards, with a confident mind, she carried it with her to the people assembled to watch the case, along with the wicked tyrant. She then produced the silver brooch for them to see, with many who knew the piece of jewelry testifying that it was none other than the same brooch under discussion. Thus the chaste maiden was set free from the hands of the cruel tyrant. And afterwards he humbly confessed his crime to holy Brigid with neck bowed. And she, glorified by all for carrying out this great miracle, giving thanks to God and doing everything for his glory, returned to her home.

19 Num 35:6–32; Josh 20:1–9.
20 A common motif in folklore, as in the story of the ring of Polycrates (Herodotus 3.40–3). A similar story is also found in Mt 17:24–7.

26. And to these miracles ought to be added her glorious and most celebrated stay with a certain faithful woman. For holy Brigid was making a prosperous journey according to the will of God in wide Mag Breg, when the day passed into evening. Coming upon the dwelling of this woman, she spent the night with her.

The woman welcomed her gladly with open hands and gave thanks to almighty God for the happy arrival of the most revered Brigid as if she were Christ. Since she did not have any fuel to feed the fire or food for guests, she threw into the fire as fuel the loom on which she did weaving. And on the wood of the fire she gladly lay her cow's calf which she had killed and then roasted.

And when dinner was done in praise of God, night passed with the usual vigils. Waking up afterwards in the morning, that woman, who had given up her cow's calf, in fact had suffered no loss of anything from the welcoming and feeding of holy Brigid, for she discovered another calf of the same kind with her cow which she loved as much as the previous one. And similarly the wood of the loom had been restored to her in the same form and quantity as was the earlier one.

And thus holy Brigid, with a happy turn of events and a wondrous miracle performed, said farewell to the house and its occupants and continued on her favorable journey.

27. And among the great multitude of miracles, this outstanding work by the same woman ought to be admired.

Once when three lepers oppressed by disease asked to receive some gift from her, she generously gave them a silver vessel. And lest there be any cause of discord and contention among them, she asked a certain man skilled in weighing gold and silver to divide it among them, so that between the three of them the vessel might be weighed out into three equal parts

When he began to make excuses for himself, saying that it was not possible to divide it equally, Brigid, that most cheerful of women, having grabbed the silver vessel threw it against a rock and broke it, as she wished, into three equal and similar parts.

Wondrously, when afterwards the three parts of that silver vessel were weighed and measured, not one of those three parts was discovered to be greater or lesser than another by even a single *obolus*.[21] And so the poor and sick paupers returned to their homes happy without any cause of grievance or envy among themselves.

28. Following the example of most blessed Job,[22] she never allowed the poor to go away from her without charity.

Once she gave away to the poor the foreign vestments from across the sea of the distinguished and eminent Bishop Conleth. He was accustomed to use these vestments for the solemnities[23] of the Lord and the vigils of the Apostles[24] when he offered the sacred mysteries on the altar[25] and in the sanctuary.

And when the time of the solemnity arrived, as was customary for the presiding priest of the people, he prepared to dress in his special vestments. Holy Brigid, who had earlier given away his episcopal vestments to Christ in the appearance of a poor man, substituted similar vestments of equal texture and colour that had just been given to her by Christ whom she had earlier clothed as a pauper. These vestments were brought to her in a two-wheeled chariot.

Just as she had freely given the other vestments to the poor, so she was given these new ones in their place when needed. For since she herself was a living and most blessed member of the highest ruler, she performed everything she desired with power.

21 A very small measure of weight, roughly 1/48 of a Roman ounce.
22 A 'blameless and upright man' from the book of the same name in the Hebrew Bible. Job was celebrated for his generosity in early Christian literature.
23 A major holy day of the liturgical year.
24 An evening worship service before the feast day of one of the apostles of Christ.
25 The celebration of the Eucharist in the Mass.

29. This is another outstanding deed of the same woman that cannot be passed over untold.

There was a certain poor man compelled by some need who asked her for a small amount of honey. And while Brigid was grieving in her mind because she had no portion of honey to give the man who was asking, the hum of bees was heard underneath the floor of the house where she was staying. When the place where the bees were humming was dug up and searched, she found there enough honey for the need of the man asking.

And thus when he received from her the gift of as much honey as necessity demanded, he returned to his own home rejoicing.

30. Holy Brigid also shines forth in this miracle.

One time an edict from the king of the country in which she was living came into force for the people and provinces that were under his rule declaring that in all his regions and provinces the populations and people must come together and build a wide road. It must have a solid foundation of logs and rocks and a very firm entrenchment in the deep and almost impassable bogs and in the wet and marshy places through which ran a large river. The road must be able to bear the weight of four-wheeled chariots and horsemen and carts and wagon wheels and the rush of people and an attack against enemies from all sides.

When many people had gathered together by kin groups and families, they divided the road that they had to build into sections so that each kin group and family would build their own appointed section.

And when the most difficult and laborious part by the river fell by lot to one of the tribes, they wanted to avoid that very hard labour. So by force they compelled the weaker tribe of holy Brigid to do the difficult section of road construction. And this cruel and unjust tribe picked an easier section than the one they had been assigned by lot. This section they would build without any difficulty caused by the river.

And when holy Brigid's kin according to the flesh came to her complaining and beaten down by the stronger tribe without any recourse to justice, it is said that she told them, 'Go away! It rests with the will and power of God that the river move from the place where it is and where hard labour is wearing you down to the place chosen'.

And when in the morning all the people had risen to work, that river that they were complaining about was seen to have left its course and bed of old where it used to flow between two banks and to have moved from the part where the tribe of holy Brigid was compelled to work into the part of the stronger and prideful people who had unjustly forced the smaller and weaker tribe to labour with greatest difficulty.

And as testimony of this miracle, the vestiges of the river and the empty channel where the flowing and gushing river used to be in the past appears today as a dry place without any moving water, the river having moved to another place.

31. Not only did she work many miracles in her mortal life before she put away her body, but she did not cease afterwards to perform other miracles at the monastery where her venerable body rests by the generosity of the divine gift. These miracles we not only have heard about but seen with our own eyes.

For the abbot of the greatest and most famous monastery of holy Brigid, whom I briefly mentioned earlier in this little book, ordered workers and stonecutters to seek out and cut a millstone from whatever place they might be able to find one.

And these men set out without any previous knowledge of the paths, climbing a very difficult and steep route. They chose a large stone on the very summit of a mountain and, cutting it all the way around, they shaped it into a circular and perforated millstone.

And when the abbot from the monastery at their invitation had come with oxen and men to that mountain where the millstone had been shaped, he was not able to drag or drive the oxen because of the steep ascent up the mountain. Indeed he was scarcely able to make the difficult assent himself with a few men following him.

Then he with his companions and the workmen tried to think of a way they might move that millstone from the ridge of the high mountain since there was no way on that steep slope of the mountain that oxen could be yoked and pull that load. Then in despair about the task, with some of the men already leaving and abandoning the stone that those who had worked it had made in vain, the abbot with prudent thought and counsel faithfully said to his workers, 'Let this not be done, but instead lift up the stone with courage and roll it down the slope from this highest peak of the mountain, invoking the name and power of most revered holy Brigid. Because we by no skill or strength are able to carry this huge millstone through this rocky and very difficult place unless Brigid – to whom nothing is impossible, in accord with the saying that all things are possible to one believing – is able to move it to a place where the strength of the oxen will be able to pull it'.

And so with firm faith they toppled the stone and let it descend until it was rolling down the mountain by itself, sometimes swerving avoiding rocks and other times jumping over them. Then it rolled through swampy ground at the bottom of the mountain on which neither men nor oxen were able to stand. It made its miraculous journey down the mountain before them to the plain without any fragment breaking off, so that it came at last to where the oxen were waiting. And thus from there the oxen dragged it to the mill where it was skillfully joined to a second stone.

And so this millstone, which had been moved in the name of blessed Brigid, became known to everyone and this previously unknown and celebrated miracle was attributed to her.

But there was a certain pagan and heathen druid who lived in a house near that mill who deviously sent his grain to the mill with an ignorant man, its origin unknown to the miller who did the work of grinding grain. And when the grain arrived and was poured between the two grinding stones, the first stone mentioned above would not move by any means. Neither the might and power of the strong river nor the violent force of the water nor the efforts of the labourers could push it into its circular motion and accustomed movement.

And the men who saw this were troubled by it and utterly frustrated. But then discovering that the grain belonged to the druid, they had no doubt that the millstone in which holy Brigid had worked a divine miracle had refused to grind the grain of the pagan man into flour. But as soon as they took out the grain of that pagan and placed their own grain from the monastery under the stone, the normal and usual motion of the millstone was immediately restored without any difficulty.

After some time it happened that this mill was burned by fire. It was then again that no small miracle occurred, for although the building was totally consumed by flames along with the second stone, which had been joined to the one mentioned above, the fire did not dare touch in any way or burn that large millstone special to holy Brigid. But without any damage from the fire in the great burning of the mill, it remained quite unharmed.

After this, when the miracle had been seen, the millstone was carried to the monastery where it was placed with honour next to the decorated interior gate of the wall around the church where people gather to venerate the miracle of most blessed Brigid. And when the faithful touch this stone of Brigid, through which she performed the miracles mentioned above, it drives out diseases and weariness.

32. Nor can one keep quiet about the miracle of repairing the church in which the glorious bodies of both rest, that is, of Archbishop Conleth and the most flourishing virgin Brigid. They are positioned to the right and to the left of the decorated altar in tombs adorned with a variety of fashioned gold and silver and gems

and precious stones with crowns of gold and silver hanging above and different images of various carvings and colours.

And so in this ancient place something new is born – a church growing in the number of faithful of both sexes with a spacious floor and a ceiling towering far above. It is decorated with painted pictures and inside has three full oratories and is divided into sections by walls under one roof of the great church. One wall is decorated with painted images and covered with linen wall hangings along the eastern side of the church stretching from one wall of the church to the other. At either end it has two doors. Through the door positioned on the right side one enters into the sanctuary to the altar, where the presiding priest with his monks and those appointed to the sacred mysteries offer the Lord's sacred sacrifice. Through the other door, on the left side of the previously-mentioned transverse wall, only the abbess with her nuns and faithful widows enter to enjoy the banquet of the body and blood of Jesus Christ.

The second wall dividing the sections of the floor of the church into two equal parts extends from the eastern[26] wall to the wall running across the church. This church contains within itself many windows and a decorated door on the right side, through which the priests and the faithful of male sex enter into the church. Through another door on the left side, the nuns and the faithful women are accustomed to enter.

Thus in one grand basilica are a great many people of all ranks and social standing and sex and places of origin, with walls placed between them, differing in status but praying in one spirit to the omnipotent Master.

And when the old door of the left entryway – through which holy Brigid used to come into the church – was hung on its hinges by the workmen, it was discovered that it was not large enough to fill the new doorway. The whole bottom quarter of the entryway

26 The manuscript from Reims and several others have 'eastern' (*orientali*), but other early manuscripts have 'western' (*occidentali/occidentalis*).

showed an open gap. Only if another quarter had been added to the door would it have then filled up the space in the new entryway.

When the craftsmen were trying to decide whether they should make a whole new door to fill up the entryway or attach enough wood to the bottom of the old door to cover the gap, the previously-mentioned master, who was the greatest of all the craftsmen in Ireland, offered his prudent advice. He said, 'We should faithfully pray during the coming night beside holy Brigid so that she might reveal to us in the morning what it is that she wants us to do about this task'.

And so he spent the night praying at the glorious tomb of Brigid. And rising in the morning after that night of praying faithfully, he hung the old door back on its hinges and closed it. It now fit perfectly, being neither too large nor too small in size.

And so Brigid extended that door in height so that it filled the entryway and there was no gap visible except when it was pulled back on its hinges to enter the church. This miracle of the Lord's power was clearly revealed to the eyes of everyone who saw that door and doorway.

Who can express in words the great beauty of this church and the countless wonders of the monastic city around it, if it is right to call it a city even though it doesn't have walls surrounding it? Nonetheless, because countless people gather there – and a city is called such because many people gather there – it is a very great and metropolitan city. Holy Brigid marked out the area around it with a boundary so that it fears no human foe nor enemy. Instead it along with the surrounding area is the safest of all the cities of refuge in Ireland for those who flee to it. In it the treasuries of kings are preserved and it is seen as the most excellent because of its suitable supremacy.

Who is able to number the different crowds and countless people coming there from all the provinces? Some come for the abundant feasting, others come to be healed of their diseases, others for the spectacle of the crowds, while others bring gifts and dedications at the solemnity of the feast of holy Brigid, which is on the first day of February, the day she fell asleep and cast off the burdens of the flesh to follow the Lamb of God into the heavenly mansions.

EPILOGUE

I ask pardon from my brothers and those reading these words – and even from those emending them. I was compelled to write this book by the cause of obedience, having no special knowledge and have only skimmed over in my little boat an immense sea of miracles of holy Brigid – daunting even to the most learned men. I have recorded in my rustic speech only a few of her very great and countless miracles.

Pray for me, Cogitosus, a sinful descendant of Áed.[27] I pray that you forgive my boldness and commend me to the Lord with the shield of your prayers. And may God hear you who follow the peace of the Gospel. Amen.

Thus ends the life of holy Brigid the virgin.

---

27 Áed was a bishop of Kildare (died 639) and a member of the ruling Uí Dúnlaige family of northern Leinster.

VITA SANCTAE BRIGIDAE

Incipit vita sanctae Brigidae virginis quae est Kalendiis Febrarii.

PROLOGUS[1]

Me cogitis, fratres, ut sanctae ac beatae memoriae Brigidae virginis virtutes et opera, more[2] doctorum, memoriae litterisque tradere adgrediar. Quod opus inpositum et delicate materiae arduum paruitati et ignorantiae meae et linguae minime convenit. Sed potens est Deus de minimis magna facere, ut de exiguo olei et farinae pugillo domum inpleuit pauperculae viduae.

Itaque iussionibus vestris coactus, satis habeo meam non defuisse oboedientiam. Et ideo pauca de pluribus a maioribus ac peritissimis tradita, sine ulla ambiguitatis caligine, ne inoboedientiae crimen incurram, patefacere censeo.

Ex quibus quanta qualisque virgo virtutum bonarum florida cunctorum oculis innotescat. Non quod memoria et mediocritas et rusticus sermo ingenioli mei tanti muneris officium explicare valeret. Sed fidei vestrae beatitudo et orationum vestrarum diuturnitas meretur accipere quod non valet ingenium ferre dictantis.

Haec ergo egregiis crescens virtutibus et fama bonarum rerum, ad eam de omnibus prouinciis totius Hiberniae innumerabiles populi de utroque sexu confluentes et vota sibi vouentes voluntariae, suum monasterium caput paene omnium Hybernensium ecclesiarum et culmen praecellens omnia monasteria Scotthorum, cuius parroechia per totam Hybernensem terram defusa a mari usque ad mare extensa est. In campestribus campi Liffei[3] supra fundamentum fidei firmum construxit.

1 *omit* BBr
2 *omit* LRnS, morum R, more BgN
3 lyfei CLRn, liphei Bg, lifei MN

Et prudenti dispensatione de animabus suorum regulariter in omnibus procurans et de ecclesiis multarum prouintiarum sibi adherentibus sollicitans, et secum reuoluens quod sine summo sacerdote qui ecclesias consecraret et ecclesiasticos in eis gradus subrogaret esse non posse. Inlustrem virum et solitarium Conleh[4] et omnibus moribus bonis ornatum per quem Deus virtutes operatus est plurimas, conuocans eum de heremo et de sua vita solitaria, et in ipsius obuiam pergens, ut ecclesiam in episcopali dignitate cum ea gubernaret atque ut nihil de ordine sacerdotali in suis deesset ecclesiis accessiuit.

Et sic postea uctum[5] caput et principale omnium episcoporum et beatissima puellarum[6] principalis felici comitatu inter se et gubernaculis omnium virtutum suam rexerunt principalem ecclesiam. Et amborum meritis suam cathedram[7] episcopalis et puellaris acsi vitis fructifera diffusa undique ramis crescentibus in totam Hybernensi insula inoleuit. Quam semper archiepiscopus Hybernensium episcoporum abbatissam quam omnes abbatisse Scothorum venerantur, felici successione et ritu perpetuo dominantur.

Exinde ego[8] ut supra dixi a fratribus coactus, beatae huius Brigidae virtutes tam eas quae ante principatum, quamque alias[9] gessit, tanto studio breuitatis, licet praepostero ordine virtutum, conpendiose explicare conabor.[10]

Explicit praefatio de sanctae Brigidae virtutibus.[11]

1.[12] Sancta itaque Brigida, quam Deus presciuit ad suam imaginem et predestinauit, a Christianis nobilibusque parentibus[13] de bona ac

4   *omit* CLRnS, nomine conleeth BgN
5   unicum RBBr
6   *omit* omnium ... principalis RBBr, omnium episcoporum et beatissimarum puellarum OP$_1$CLBgMNP$_2$P$_3$Rn
7   sua cathedra OP$_1$BgM
8   ergo OBgN
9   *insert* quas in principatu OP$_1$CMP$_2$P$_3$
10   *omit* P$_1$CLMRnS
11   *omit* explicit ... virtutibus P$_1$CLMNRnS.
12   *insert* chapter titles R

prudentissima Ectech[14] prosapia in Scothia orta, patreque Dubtacho[15] et matre Brocca[16] genita. A sua pueritia bonarum rerum studiis inoleuit. Electa enim ex Deo puella moribus sobria aetatis ac pudicitiae plena in meliora semper crescebat.

Et quis sua opera ac virtutes quae etiam in hac aetate gessit plene enarrare valet? Sed haec pauca et de innumerabilibus exempli causa posita demonstrabimus.

Ex inde haec cum tempus maturum aduenit in opus coagli ut de turbato vaccarum lacte butyrum congregaret a matre transmissa est. Ut sicut aliae feminae hoc opus exercere solebant, ipsa quoque aequali modo perageret, et ut cum ceteris in tempore placito vaccarum fructum ac pondus mensuratumque butyri solitum plenissime in usum redderet.

Sed haec moribus pulcherrima et hospitalis virgo, oboedire magis volens Deo quam hominibus, pauperibus et hospitibus lac largiter et butyrum distribuit.

Et cum secundum morem oportunum aduenit tempus ut omnes redderent fructum vaccarum ad eam peruentum est. Et cum cooperatrices eius monstrabant sua opera completa, quaesitum est a beata supradicta virgine ut est ipsa similiter adsignaret suum opus.

Et ipsa matris timore pauida cum non haberet quod monstraret quia totum pauperibus erogauit crastinum non procurans tempus. Tanta et inextinguibili flamma fidei accensa ac firma, ad Dominum se conuertens orauit.

Nec mora Dominus vocem virginis audiens ac praeces, largitate diuini muneris, sicut est adiutor in oportunitatibus, adfuit. Et pro sua in se virgine confidenti, afluenter butyrum restituit.

Mirum in modum et illa hora post orationem virgo sanctissima nihil de suo opere deesse ostendens, sed super omnes cooperatrices habundas se monstrauit complesse suum officium.

13 *omit* a christianis nobilibusque parentibus P₁CLBgMNRn
14 *omit* P₁CLBgMNRnS, ectehe Br
15 dubtocho BBrOP₁CBgMP₂P₃Rn, duptocho Rn, dabtoch Bg
16 processa Br, broccha O, broicsech nomina P₁, chrocha Bg

Et cum plenissime inuentum in oculis omnium tanti muneris miraculum innotuit et laudantes Deum qui hoc fecit tantam fidei virtutem in virginali pectore constitisse admirati sunt.

2. Ac non multo post cum eam sui parentes, more humano, viro desponsare volebant. Illa caelitus inspirata se virginem castam exhibere Deo volens, ad episcopum sanctissimum beate memoriae Mac Caille[17] perrexit. Qui caeleste intuens desiderium et pudicitiam et tantum castitatis amorem in tali virgine, pallium album et vestem candidam super ipsius venerabile caput inposuit.

Quae coram Deo et episcopo ac altari genua humiliter flectens et suam virginalem coronam Domino omnipotenti offerens, fundamen ligneum, quo altare fulciebatur, manu tetigit.

Quod lignum in comemoratione pristinae virtutis usque ad praesens tempus viride ac si non esset excisum et decorticatum, sed in radicibus fixum, virescit. Et usque hodie languores et morbos de omnibus expellit fidelibus.

3. Nec praetereundum mihi videtur commemorare de illa virtute quam haec famosissima famula Dei ac diuino incessanter famulatui tradita operata est.

Nam cum illa aliquando in caldaria lardam aduenientibus hospitibus coxerat, cani adulanti ac flagitanti misericorditer eam tradidit.

Et cum larda de caldaria tracta ac postea hospitibus esset diuisa acsi non esset dempta plenissime reperta est.

Et valde hi qui hoc viderunt admirantes puellam incompar-abilem virtute fidei et merito bonarum virtutum dignis laudibus diuulgauerunt.

4. Et eadem messores ac operarios conuocauit in messem suam. Et facta illa messorum conuentione, nebulosa ac pluuialis dies illa accidit conuentionis et pluuiis largiter ex nubibus effusis per totam illam in circuitu prouintiam. Ac riuulis guttarum affluentia per

17 machellem Br, machille CLBgMNRnS, maccaire P₂

conualles et rimas terrarum currentibus, sua messis sola arida sine pluuiarum inpedimento et turbatione perstitit.

Et cum omnes messores ipsius undique regionis pluuiali die prohibiti essent, sui sine ulla umbra caliginis pluuie illa die tota ab ortu usque ad occasum solis messure Dei potentia opus exercebant.

5.[18] Ecce inter ceteras virtutes ipsius, hoc opus dignum admiratione videtur esse et admirabile.

Aduenientibus enim episcopis et cum ea hospitantibus, cum non haberet unde eos cibaret, adiuta Dei multiplici virtute, solito more, habundanter ut sua poscebat necessitas.

Vaccam unam eandemque tribus contra consuetudinem in una die vicibus mulsit. Et quod solet de optimis tribus vaccis exprimi, ipsa, mirabili euentu, de una sua expressit vacca.

6. Ecce et hanc virtutem, beatitudini vestrae, insinuare censeo, in qua mens pura virginalis et manus cooperatrix diuina in unum apparent conuenire.

Nam haec cum suas opere pastorali pasceret oues in campestri et herboso loco, largitate nimia pluuiarum perfusa humidis vestibus domum rediit.

Et cum umbra solaris per foramina domum intrinsecus intraret, illam umbram, obtusa oculorum acie, arborem fuisse transuersam et fixam putans ac desuper suam complutam vestem ponens, tamquam in arbore grandi et firma in ipso tenui solari umbraculo vestis pependit.

Et cum ipsius domus habitatores et vicini, hoc ingenti fuissent miraculo perculsi, hanc incomparabilem dignis laudibus extollebant.

7. Et hoc silentio opus non est pretereundum.

Cum enim haec sancta Brigida in agro iuxta gregem ouium pascendum, cura pastorali esset sollicita, aliquis nequam adolescens callide subripiens et ipsius largitatem in pauperes conprobans, et mutato semper habitu ad eam septies veniens, septem ab ea veruices in una detulit die et in secreto abscondit.

18 *omit* Br

Et cum grex ad vesperum et ex more ad caulas fuerat dirigendus, duabus vel tribus vicibus diligentissime adnumeratus, sine damno sui mirum in modum totus integro reppertus est numero.

Et admirantes hi qui conscii facti fuerant, virtutem Dei manifeste factam per virginem, septem quos absconderunt veruices ad suum dimiserunt gregem. Et ille gregis numerus nec plus nec minus sed ut ante integer repertus est.

His et aliis innumerabilibus virtutibus, famosissima haec famula Dei in ore omnium super omnes non inmerito sed dignis laudibus excellentissima visa est.

8. Mirabili quoque euentu ab hac venerabili Brigida leprosi ceruisam flagitantes. Cum non haberet illa, videns aquam ad balnea paratam et cum virtute fidei benedicens in optimam conuertit ceruisam et abundanter sitientibus exhausit.

Ille enim qui in chana galileae aquam conuertit in vinum, per huius quoque beatissime feminae fidem, aquam mutauit in ceruisam.

Dum autem de hac virtute dictum est, de alia admirabili commemorationem facere aptum videtur.

9. Potentissima enim et ineffabili fidei fortitudine, aliquam feminam, post votum integritatis, fragilitate humana in iuuenali voluntatis[19] desiderio lapsam et habentem pregnantem ac tumescentem vuluam fideliter benedixit. Et euanescens in vulua conceptus, sine partu et sine dolore eam sanam ad penitentiam restituit.

Et secundum quod omnia possibilia sunt credentibus, sine ulla inpossibilitate innumera cotidie miracula operabatur.

10. Quadam enim die cum quidam ad eam salem petens veniret, sicut ceteri pauperes et egeni innumerabiles venire solebant pro suis necessitatibus, ipsa beatissima brigida in illa hora salem factum de lapide quem benedixit in opus poscentis sufficienter largita est.

Et sic ab ea salem portans laetus propriam domum rediit.

19 voluptans Br, voluptatis CLNP$_2$

11. Et hoc potentissimum opus eiusdem diuinum iungendum esse mihi videtur inter cetera quo, saluatoris instar, imitatrix diuini nominis excelsissimam operata est virtutem. Nam secundum exemplum Domini et haec oculos ceci aperuit nati. Sua enim nomina et opera membris Dominus largitus est suis.

Quia cum de semetipso loqueretur, 'Ego sum lux mundi' nihilominus suis dicit apostolis, 'Vos estis lux mundi' et de hisdem idem dicens intulit, 'Opera quae ego facio et ipsi facient et maiora horum facient'.

Inde quem naturalis partus caecum protulit natum, fides eiusdem Brigide grano comparata sinapis et consimilis eidem oculos simplices et lucidos ingenti miraculo aperuit.

12. Haec itaque tantis virtutibus inlustris humilitate cordis et puritate mentis et morum temperantia ac spirituali gratia plena, tantam auctoritatem in diuino cultu et celebre nomen prae omnibus coaetaneis virginibus habere meruit.

Et quadam die cum una ex adherentibus sibi extrinsecus femina cum filia duodecim annos aetatis, ex naturali procreatione muta, ad eam veniret visitandam cum digna reuerentia, ut omnes solebant, se inclinans et humili collo ad eius pacificum osculum procidens.

Ipsa omnibus affabilis Brigida ac felix conditis sale diuino sermonibus eam salubriter allocuta est ac saluatoris nostri exemplo iubentis paruulos ad se venire, filiae manum retinens manu sua, nesciente illa quod esset muta, et voluntatem ipsius interrogans utrum velato capite permanere virgo annuptus tradenda esse vellet.

Matre ipsius admonente quod sibi filia nulla daret responsa, respondens matri dixit se non dimissuram filiae manum nisi sibi prius responsum redderet. Et cum filiam secunda vice interrogaret de eadem respondit filia sibi, dicens, 'Non aliud nisi quod tu volueris agere volo'.

Ac sic postea aperto ore sine lingue inpedimento et soluto ipsius vinculo sana loquebatur.

13. Et quibus hoc eiusdem opus nullis[20] multorum auribus antea inauditum scrupulum non moueret?

Cum enim haec animo esset intenta caelestium meditatione ut semper solebat suam de terrestribus ad caelestia eleuans conuersationem,[21] quamdam non paruam sed grandem lardi partem cum cane dimisit. Et cum esset inquisita, non alicubi sed in loco ubi canis solebat esse, mense transacto, intacta et integra reperta est.

Non enim canis ausus est comedere depositum beate virginis, sed custos patiens lardi et idoneus, contra suum solitum morem, diuina refrenatus virtute et domitus extitit.

14.[22] Et crescente cotidie miraculorum numero, quae vix enumerari possunt, quantum misericordie et pietatis et in pauperes elymosinarum oportune et inoportune postulantium operata est.

Nam cum aliquis indigens cibo pauperum eam rogaret, illa ad eos qui carnes coxerant ut ab illis aliquid pauperi deferret festinauit. Et illorum unus stolidissimus famulus qui carnes coxerat insipienter partem nondum carnis coctam in albatum ipsius sinuate vestis receptaculum transiecit. Et sic illa non suffuscato mantili sed in suo candido colore manente portans pauperi tribuit.

15. Nec non et hoc de eius gestis felicibus admirari debet.

Confluentibus enim ad eam undique pauperibus et peregrinis ingenti fama virtutum et nimie largitatis tracti, accedens inter eos ingratus quidam leprosus optimam de armento vaccam cum optimo vitulo omnium vitulorum in simul sibi donari poscebat.

Nec ipsa eius audiens preces[23] distulit, sed mox illam quam optimam didicit de omnibus vaccam et alicuius vaccae vitulum eligantem et optimum roganti infirmo voluntarie donauit.

Et misericorditer suum cum illo transmittens currum per iter longum et latissimum campum ne molestiam in vacca minanda

20 *omit* B, *insert* non BrP₁CMNRn
21 *omit* ut … conuersationem P₁CLMRn
22 *omit* Br
23 *insert* non CLM

infirmus longo fessus itinere sustentaret. Vitulum post tergum eius in currum poni precipiebat.

Et sic eum vacca lingua tangens et tamquam proprium diligens nemine eam cogente, usque ad loca destinata consecuta est.

Karissimi videtis fratres quod et bruta contra consuetudinem famulabantur ei animalia.

16. Et quodam interuallo temporis alii nequissimi fures qui nec Deum nec homines verebantur de alia prouintia ob latrocinium venientes et per amnem grandem facili meatu pedum egredientes, boues[24] ipsius furati sunt.

Sed eos eadem reuertentes via impetus ingentis fluminis inundatione aquarum subita facta conturbauit. Non enim flumen instar muri erectum scelestissimam boum fraudem beatae Brigidae per se transire[25] permisit, sed eos fures demergens et secum trahens boues de ipsorum manibus liberati loris in cornibus pendentibus ad proprium armentum ac boellium reuersi sunt.

17. Ecce et hic virtus diuina apparet.

Cum quadam die ipsa sanctissima Brigida, cogente aliqua utilitatis necessitate, conuentionem plebis visitaret in curru sedens in equis binis vehebatur. Et eum in suo vehiculo meditatione theorica caelestem agens in terris vitam suum, ut solebat, dominatorem oraret de alto procidens.

Loco alter bruto animo equus saliens sub curru et inrefrenatus habenis fortiter se extorquens et de iugo semetipsum absoluens, equo altero solo sub suo remanente iugo, exterritus per campestria cucurrit.

Et sic manus diuina iugum pendens sine precipitio sustentans, et vidente turba ob testimonium virtutis diuinae, secura in suo orans vehiculo cum uno equo sub curru posito, ad plebis conuentionem discursu placabili inlesa peruenit. Et sic signis et virtutibus suam

24 bouem BOP$_2$
25 *insert* non BrP$_1$LRn

confirmans doctrinam, sermonibus salutaribus et sale divino
conditis plebem hortata est.

18. Et hoc virtutibus ipsius videtur nobis esse deputandum.

Cum aper ferus singularis et siluestris territus et fugitiuus esset
ad gregem porcorum Brigidae felicissimae concitus cursu praecipiti
peruenit. Quem ipsa euentu inter suas cernens sues benedixit.
Deinde inpauidus ac familiaris cum ipsius permansit grege
porcorum.

Ecce videtis, fratres, quod et bruta animalia et bestiae sermonibus
et voluntati eius resistere non poterant, sed domita et subiecta sibi
famulabantur.

19. Nam cum aliquando aliquis inter ceteros offerentes ei munera,
de longa veniens prouincia offerret sues pingues et alios secum
missos ire ad suam villam quodam longo terrarum interuallo
positam rogaret ut ab eo sues acciperent. Per longum itineris
spatium dierum trium vel quatuor amplius prolixum cum eo suos
missos transmisit comites.

Ac transacto unius diei itinere in monte confinali regionum, qui
proprio nuncupatur vocabulo Gabor,[26] suaes suas quas in longinquis
opinabantur esse regionibus, obuias contra se venire a lupis directas
per viam et coactas contemplati sunt.

Et cum ille cuius erant intellexisset suas esse, agnoscens sues
proprias et videret agrestes lupi, qui ob maximam beate Brigide
reuerentiam de siluis maximis et campo Liffei latissimo[27] idonei
pastores in coactis et minandis suibus laborabant, aduenientibus
missis relinquentes eas inlesas, mirabilique hoc agentes intellectu et
consueto more discesserunt.

Et sic altero die hi qui missi erant cum suibus factum mirabile
narrantes domum reuersi sunt.

---

26 grabor Br, cabor CLMRn, gabor liphi P₁

27 campos ea elatissimo R, campo liffei latissimos BO, campeo lei latissimo Br, campo
   lifei latissimo P₁CLMRnS

20. Item de eiusdem mirabilibus gestis hoc factum videtur nobis minime praeter eundum enarrari.

Quadam enim die cum aliquis nulla subfultus scientia vulpem per regis palatium ambulantem videret, putans illam obcaecatis sensibus suis feram esse bestiam, et quod aulam regis familiaris et mansueta esset, variis artibus docta agilitate corporis et subtilitate animi regi et suis comitibus grande praestans spectaculum ignoraret, vidente multitudine, occidit eam.

Et tunc ab his qui viderunt factum alligatus et diffamatus, ad regem perductus est. Et rex iratus rem discens gestam, nisi sibi vulpis similis in omnibus calliditatibus quas sua vulpis operabatur, restituta esset, illum iussit occidi et uxorem et filios suos et omnia quae habuit in seruitutem redigi praecepit.

Et cum rem gestam sancta ac venerabilis Brigida didicisset, tanto misericordiarum et pietatis affectu permota, currum suum sibi iungi praecipiens et ex intimo corde dolens pro ipso infelici qui iniuste iudicatus est praecibus ad Dominum profusis et per planitiem campi equitans perrexit in viam quae ad regis palatium ducebatur.

Nec mora Dominus exaudiens ipsam suas fundentem assiduas praeces unam de suis vulpibus feris ad eam venire transmisit, quae cum velocissimo cursu per campestria veniret et beatissimae Brigidae currui appropinquaret, leuiter se eleuans in currum intrauit et sub receptaculo vestis Brigidae se constituens, sobrie cum ea in curru sedebat.

At cum ipsa ad regem veniret ut ille miser inprouidus qui illo reatu suae ignorantiae tenebatur liber et absolutus de vinculis egrederetur coepit precari. Et cum rex eius praecibus consentire noluisset obtestans se non illum dimissurum nisi talem vulpem tantae mansuetudinis et calliditatis qualis vulpis sua fuerat restituta sibi esset, ipsa suam protulit in medium vulpem, quae coram rege et omni multitudine totos mores et subtilitatem docibilem alterius agens vulpis in eadem forma prioris palam omnibus variis lusit artibus.

Et tunc rex haec videns placatus et eius optimates cum ingenti plausu admirantis multitudinis mirabile factum illum solui et liberum abire qui fuerat antea reus delicti iussit.

Nec multo post cum sancta Brigida solutione ipsius et libertate facta ad suam remearet domum, ipsa vulpis dolosa se inter turbas torquens et callide mouens quae ut altera omnibus videbatur similis fugitiua ad loca deserta et siluestria ad suum antrum multis sequentibus et canibus se persequentibus inludens ac per patentes campos fugiens incolumis euasit.

Et omnes admirantes hoc quod factum fuerat priuilegio sanctitatis et praerogatiua virtutum multarum semper pollentem maioribus gestis sanctam venerati sunt Brigidam.

21. Et cum in alia die anates pectore carnali natantes in aqua et per aera interdum volitantes beata vidisset Brigida, eas ad se venire accerrsiuit. Quae pinnigero volatu et tanto ardore oboedientiae eius vocibus tamquam sub humana cura essent consuetae sine ulla formidine multitudines ad eam volitabant.

Quas manu tangens et amplectens et per aliquantulum temporis hoc idem faciens, redire ac volare suis in aerem alis permisit. Conlaudans creatorem omnium rerum inuisibilem per creaturas visibiles cui omnia subiecta sunt animantia et cui omnia viuunt, ut quidam ait officio gerendi.

Et ex his omnibus manifeste intelligi potest quod omnis natura bestiarum et pecorum et volucrum subiecta eius fuit imperio.

22. Et hoc eiusdem miraculum omnibus saeculis celebrandum auribus fidelium insinuandum est.

Nam cum semina saluberrima verbi Dominici ex more suae consuetudinis omnibus seminaret, vidit nouem viros in forma quadam speciali vanae et diabolicae superstitionis et plausum habentes vocis ridiculae ac insaniam mentis maximam. In quorum vis contritio erat et infelicitas, qui antiquo hosti qui in illis regnabat, votis scelestissimis et iuramentis sitientes effusionem sanguinis, antequam kalendae illius[28] mensis superuenirent venturi aliorum iugulationem et homicidia facere disposuerunt.

Quibus reuerentissima et affabilis Brigida melliflua verborum copia praedicauit, ut mortiferis erroribus relictis sua crimina per cordis conpunctionem et veram delerent paenitentiam. Qui hebetudine mentis suae nisi prius vana sua conplessent vota illud facere resistentes in viam suam perrexerunt. Et pro hac re fusis ad Dominum praecibus assiduis decoratae virginis volentis Domini exemplo omnes saluos fieri et ad agnitionem venire veritatis.

Et egredientes illi nefarii, imaginem instar viri quem debuissent iugulare contemplantes et continuo suis iugulantes lanceis et gladiis decollantes, quasi post triumphum de suorum aduersario et inimico cum armis sanguineis et cruentis reuersi multis apparuerunt.

Mirum in modum, cum neminem occiderent, illis visum est sua complesse vota. Atque cum nemo deerat de illa prouincia de quo illi triumpharent, nulla dubietas pro hac re alicui persistens, largitas muneris diuini per sanctam Brigidam facta omnibus innotuit. Et sic illi, qui antea erant homicidae, per penitentiam ad Dominum conuersi sunt.

23. Et in hoc opere per decoratam Brigidam cultu inenarrabili sacrae religionis diuina manifestata est potentia.

Illam enim Luguidma[29] nomine validus vir valde et virorum fortissimus, xii virorum opera per semetipsum tanta fortitudine sui corporis in una, cum vellet, laborans die et cibaria quibus xii sufficienter viri vesci possint similiter comedens. Sicut enim illorum opera facere solus sic et cibaria aequali modo unus contra plures comedere poterat.

Deprecatus est ut pro se Dominum oraret omnipotentem ut eius ingluuiem qua superflua deuorabat temperaret, nec antiquam virtutem sui corporis pro hac amisisset.

28 iulii OBr, illis B
29 luguidmam BP$_2$, quidam enim vir luguid Br, quidam enim vir validus P$_1$

Et sic ipsa causa Brigida illum benedicens et pro illo Dominum orans ipse postea victu unius viri satis contentus ac ut antea solebat, laborans sicut xii operarii operabatur, in eadem antiquam permansit virtutem.

24. Item inter eius opera praeclara hoc idem egregium opus et excelsum compertumque omnibus explicare debemus.

Arbor quaedam grandis et maxima ad aliquem parata usum ab omnibus qui artificia exercere solebant in silua lignorum securibus excisa est. Ad quam conuentio virorum fortium propter eius molestiam et ingentem molem et loca difficillima hi quibus ramorum cum fragore suorum ruit ut deponeret ac traherent cum multis bubus et artificum machinis ad locum destinatum ut necessitas rei poscebat congregata est.

Et cum nec multitudo virorum nec vires boum et variae artificum artes mouere vel trahere eam arborem ullo modo poterant, recedentibus cunctis ab ea per fortissimam fidem beatae Brigidae grano sinapis similem, per quam fidem ut magister caelestis organo euangelicae vocis docet montes mutantur sicut possibilia sunt omnia credentibus, eam grauissimam arborem angelicae virtutis per diuina ministeria nullo mortalium auxilio leuantes sine ulla difficultate ad locum quem voluit sancta Brigida destinatum detulerunt.

Ac per omnes prouincias tanta virtutis divinae huius excellentia deuulgata est.

25. Et nostro occurrit animo non excludere et hanc virtutem silentio nostro quam inter innumerabiles virtutes caeteras eadem operata est Brigida venerabilis.

Quidam enim vir saecularis et gente nobilis et dolosis moribus, exardescens in alicuius feminae concupiscentiam et quomodo eius concubitu frui possit callide cogitans. Ac suam sentem argenteam pretiosamque in depositum sibi commendat quam dolose retraxit ille illa ignorante et eiecit in mare ut cum ipsa non posset reddere sibi esset ancilla et eius postea uteretur ut vellet amplexibus.

Machinatus est hoc perficere malum, nulla alia re ac redemptione placatu se fieri posse dicens nisi aut propria sibi sente argentea reddita aut ipsa femina in seruitutem ei redacta pro causa culpabili fragilis concupiscentiae uteretur.

Et haec timens pudica femina tamquam ad ciuitatem refugii tutissimam ad sanctam confugit Brigidam. Quae cum talem comperisset causam vel quid pro hac re agere debuerit cogitaret cum necdum verba complesset superuenit ad se quidam cum piscibus de flumine tractis. Et cum illorum ilia piscium excisa et aperta fuissent sentis illa argentea quam ille crudelis iaecit in mare ob causam supra dictam, in medio unius ex piscibus reperta est.

Et sic postea secura mente eam sentem secum portabat et ad conuentum multitudinis pro hac culpa cum tyranno infami progrediens et monstrans sibi suam propriam sentem multis testantibus qui eam agnoscere poterant, non aliam esse sed ipsam de qua talis sermo ferebatur, adherentem sibi feminam pudicam de manibus tyranni crudelissimi liberauit. Et sic ille postea confitens suam culpam sanctae Brigidae humiliter sua subdidit colla. Et illa, ab omnibus gloriosa peracto hoc ingenti miraculo, gratias agens Deo et omnia in eius gloriam faciens, domum redit propriam.

26. Et his miraculis gloriosum eius et clarissimum cum aliqua fideli femina hospicium in iungi debet, quo prosperum iter faciens sancta Brigida in Dei voluntate in amplissimo campo Breg[30] cum declinaret ad vesperum dies, ad habitaculum eius veniens cum ea pernoctauit.

Quae obuiis manibus et gratulanter suscipiens et gratias omnipotenti agens Deo de felice aduentu reuerendissimae Brigidae tamquam Christi, cum non haberet propter suam inopiam unde ignem nutriret et cybum unde tales hospites cibaret incidens ligna telaria in quibus textura telarum operabatur in pastum ignis vitulum suae quem occidit vaccae super struem istorum ponens lignorum igni assauit cum bona voluntate.

30 *omit* P₁CLM

Et caena in Dei laudibus facta et nocte adsuetis transacta vigiliis, expergescentes post illam de mane noctem ut nullum de receptione et refectione sanctae Brigidae ullius rei sustineret damnum ipsa hospitalis, quae vitulum suae amiserat vaccae, alterum in eadem forma vitulum cum sua inuenit vacca quem ut priorem ipsa dilexerat. Et telaria ligna similiter sibi pro ceteris reparata in tali forma in quantitate in qua priora fuerant contemplata est.

Et sic sancta Brigida, felici progressu et mirabili facta virtute, domui et habitatoribus valedicens pacifice in viam suam perrexit prosperam.

27. Et ecce in tanta miraculorum multitudine hoc eiusdem opus praeclarum admirari solet.

Tribus enim leprosis et infirmitatibus oppressis, postulantibus munus aliquodcumque ab ea accipere, vas largita est argenteum. Et ne illis esset causa discordiae et contentionis, si illi inter se diuiderent cuidam in ponderibus auri et argenti conperto dixit, ut inter illos hoc vas tres ponderaret tribus aequalibus partibus.

Cum excusare se coepisset, dicens ponderare aequaliter non posse, ipsa felicissima feminarum Brigida, adprehenso vase argenteo, ipsum allidit contra lapidem et confregit in tres, ut voluit, aequales et consimiles partes.

Mirum in modum cum postea ipse tres partes ipsius vasis argentei in pondere essent emensae, nulla pars alia minor vel maior, quae aliam superaret licet uno obolo de his inuenta est tribus partibus. Et sic sui infirmi pauperes sine ulla iniuriae et inuidiae causa inter se laeti cum suis recesserunt donis.

28. Secundum enim Iob[31] exemplum beatissimi numquam inopes a se recedere sinu vacuo passa est.

Nam vestimenta transmarina et peregrina episcopi Conleath[32] decorati culminis, quibus in solemnitatibus Domini et in vigiliis

31 ipsius CLMRnS, ipsius exemplum euangelii beatissimi virgo P₁
32 concolaido Br, collodi P₁, conlei CMRnS, cumleath P₂

apostolorum sacra in altaribus et in sanctuario offerens misteria utebatur pauperibus largita est.

Et cum tempus sollemnitatis aduenit secundum consuetudinem ut ipse summus populorum pontifex suis indutus esset mutatoriis vestibus, sancta Brigida, quae priora vestimenta illius aepiscopi pro Christo in forma pauperis posito donabat, alia similia per omnia vestimenta prioribus, tam texturis quam coloribus, quae in illa hora a Christo quem per pauperem induebat, perlata sibi in curru duarum acceperat rotarum, tradidit pro aliis.

Voluntarie autem alia pauperibus vestimenta obtulit et haec pro eis oportune recepit. Nam cum ipsa esset viuum et felicissimum summi capitis membrum, potenter omnia quae desiderabat operabatur.

29. Nam et hoc eiusdem opus egregium non est praetereundum enarrari.

Quidam enim conpulsus quadam necessitate indigens mellis sextarium eam praecatus est. Et cum ipsa Brigida mente doleret, dum non haberet paratum mel quod illi roganti donaret, murmur apium vocum sub pauimento domus in qua ipsa fuerat tunc exauditum est. Et cum ille locus in quo suis apes sonabant vocibus perfossus et scrutatus fuisset, repertum est in eo quantum sufficiebat in opus poscentis.

Et sic ille ab ea recepto mellis munere quantum sibi necessitas poscebat ad sua gaudens reuersus est habitacula.

30. Item et hoc sancta fulsit Brigida miraculo.

Quia cum regis illius patriae in qua ipsa fuit edictum per plebes et prouincias, quae sub eius erant ditione et iugo, inualesceret, ut de omnibus eius regionibus et prouinciis omnes populi et plebes conuenirent atque aedificarent viam latam et firmam ramis arborum petris infundamen positis et munitionibus quibusdam firmissimis in gronna profunda et pene intransmeabili et in locis humentibus atque in paludibus in quibus grandis currebat fluuius, quae constructa quadrigas et aequites et currus et plaustrorum rotas et impetum populorum atque concursum undique hostium sustentare posset.

Conuenientibus multis populis per cognationes et familias, diuiserunt viam illam quam aedificare debuerant in partes proprias, ut unaquaeque cognatio et familia suam sibi creditam construxisset partem.

Et cum illa pars fluminis difficillima et laboriosa in sorte alicuius ex ipsis nationibus cederet euentu, ipsa natio durissimum deuitans laborem per suam fortitudinem sanctae Brigidae infirmiorem coegit nationem, ut hanc operaretur difficilem partem in structura viae et suam quam faciliorem euentu habebat partem eligens ipsa crudelis et iniusta natio aedificaret sine ulla fluminis turbatione.

Atque cum ad sanctam Brigidam suis secundum carnem cognati venissent querellosi prostratique a fortioribus sine ullo iure dispensationis,[33] ipsa illis probabiliter dixisse fertur, 'Abite. Voluntatis Dei est et potestas, ut ille fluuius transeat de loco in quo est et ubi vos dura opprimunt opera, in illam quam ipsi elegerunt partem'.

Et cum de mane ipsius diei omnes surrexissent ad opera populi, fluuius ille quem querebantur visus est reliquisse suum antiquum locum et conuallem ubi inter ambas currere solebat ripas, et transmutasse de parte ubi sanctae Brigidae natio compulsa operabatur in illorum fortium et superborum partem qui alios pauciores et infirmiores se iniuste et durissime operari conpellebant.

Et in testimonium virtutis, vestigia fluminis et vallis vacua ubi in undans et emanans antiquo currebat fluuius tempore, ipso ad alterum flumine recedente locum, ipse locus siccatus sine ullis apparet fluitantibus aquis.

31.[34] Non solum autem in sua vita carnali antequam sarcinam deponeret carnis virtutes operata est plurimas, sed largitas diuini

33 *insert* se dicerent afflici R
34 P₁CLMRnS *stop here and begin again midway through Chapter 31 following* tunc facta desperatione

muneris in suo monasterio, ubi eius venerabile requiescit corpus, alias semper operari virtutes non cessat, quas nos virtutes non solum audiuimus, sed oculis nostris vidimus.

Nam praepositus maximi et clarissimi monasterii sanctae Brigidae, de quo in huius opusculi principio breuem fecimus mentionem, operarios et lapidum caesores quaerere lapidem et incudere molarem per loca quaecumque ubi posset illi inueniri transmisit.

Et illi sine ulla prouidentia viarum difficillimam arduam ascendentes viam, ad cacumem petrosi montis perrexerunt et elegerunt lapidem grandem in ipso montis altissimi cacumine et caedentes eum de omni parte in rotundum et perforatum molarem lapidem formauerunt.

Et cum praepositus de monasterio inuitatus ab eis venisset cum bobus et viris ad illum montem in quo lapis formatus molaris atque cum boues secum propter arduam montis ascensionem trahere et cogere non possit, durissimum iter cum paucis illum sequentibus vix ascendere potuit.

Exinde ille cum suis comitibus et operariis dum cogitaret quomodo illum molarem deportarent lapidem de iugo altissimi montis, cum boues in illo praerupta montis sub oneribus et iugis esse nullo modo potuerint. Et tunc facta desperatione, aliis ex eis descendentibus illum deserere lapidem et eos in vanum laborasse qui illum formauerunt, ille praepositus prudenti dispensatione et consilio suis operariis fideliter dixit: 'Nequaquam hoc ita fiat, sed hunc leuate lapidem molarem viriliter et submittite in praecipitium de altissimo isto montis cacumine, in nomine et virtute reuerentissimae sanctae Brigidae, quia nos nullis artificiis et viribus per ista loca petrosa et difficillima hunc grandem lapidem molarem possumus portare, nisi ipsa Brigida, cui nihil inpossibile est, secundum illud quod omnia possibilia sunt credenti, illum portauerit usque ad locum, ex quo vires boum trahere ipsum possint'.

Et sic fide firma praecipitantes illum ac solum relinquentes in vallem et paulatim de monte descendens, aliquando petras deuitans, aliquando traneas ac siliens et in locis currens umidis in radice montis positis in quibus nec homines nec boues stare potuerant, pro illorum profunditate mirabili comitatu usque ad loca plana, sine ulla fragminis fractione, ubi illorum erant boues cum eis progressus est. Et ex inde ex bobus usque ad molinum vectus artificiose cum altero iunctus est lapide.

Et ut plus iste molaris lapis, qui in nomine beatae directus est Brigidae, omnibus adhuc innotesceret addidit et hoc inauditum antea et praeclarum miraculum.

Nam cum quidam paganus et gentilis ac molino vicinus suo habitaculo dolose per alium simplicem virum, ignorante molinario qui opus moliturae exercebat, suum granum ad hunc transmisisset molinum, et quodcum inter huius molares transiectum et fusum fuisset lapides, illum supradictum lapidem molarem nullus impetus fortis fluminis et directus, et nulla aquarum vis violenta, et nulla artificum conamina mouere eum ac trudere in circuitum volubilem et solitum ambitum potuerunt.

Et dum illi qui hoc viderunt de hac re cogitarent nimio perculsi stupore, tunc granum illud magi esse comperientes nullo modo dubitabant quod ille lapis molaris, in quo sancta Brigida virtutem operata est diuinam granum gentilis hominis in farinam conprimere respuisset. Et in illa hora tollentes foras granum ipsius pagani, et suum granum monasteriale subter molarem illum lapidem ponentes, cursus solitus et cotidianus sine ullis inpedimentis repentino reparatus est molae.

Et post interuallum temporis accidit ut iste molinus igni combureretur. Nec et hoc paruum fuit miraculum, cum ignis domum totam conbureret et alterum lapidem, qui iunctus supradicto lapidi fuit, hunc tantum specialem sanctae Brigidae lapidem nullo modo tangere et conburere ausus est, sed sine ulla ei molestia ignis in magno molini incendio, permansit plus incolomis.

Et postea hoc viso miraculo vectus ad monasterium perductus est et iuxta portam interioris ornati castelli quod eclesia ambitur ubi multi conueniunt populi ob uenerationem beatissimae Brigidae virtutum in ipsa porta honorifice positus est. Et de fidelibus hunc Brigidae lapidem tangentibus, per quem ipsa supradictas virtutes fecit, morbos expellit et languores.

32. Nec et de miraculo in reparatione eclesiae facto tacendum est in qua gloriosa amborum, hoc est, archiepiscopi Conleath[35] et huius virginis florentissimae Brigidae, corpora, a dextris et a sinistris altaris decorati in monumentis posita ornatis vario cultu auri et argenti et gemmarum praetiosi lapidis, atque coronis aureis et argenteis desuper pendentibus ac diuersis imaginibus cum celaturis variis et coloribus, requiescunt.

Et in veteri noua res adnascitur actu hoc est eclesia crescente numero fidelium de utroque sexu solo spatiosa et in altum minaci proceritate porrecta ac decorata pictis tabulis, tria intrinsecus habens oratoria ampla et diuisa parietibus tabulatis sub uno culmine maioris domus. In qua unus paries decoratus et imaginibus depictus ac linteaminibus tectus per latitudinem in orientali eclesiae parte a pariete ad alterum parietem aeclesiae se tetendit. Qui in suis extremitatibus duo habet in se hostia, et per unum ostium in dextra parte positum intratur in sanctuarium ad altare, ubi summus pontifex cum sua regulari scola et his quae sacris deputati sunt misteriis, sacra ac dominica immolat sacrificia. Et per alterum ostium in sinistra parte parietis supradicti et transuersi positum abbatissa cum suis puellis et viduis fidelibus tantum intrat, ut conuiuio corporis et sanguinis fruantur Ihesu Christi.

Atque alius partes pauimentum domus in duas aequales diuidens partes a pariete orientali[36] usque ad transuersum in latitudinem parietem extentus est. Et haec tenet eclesia in se multas fenestras et una in latere dextro ornatam portam, per quam sacerdotes et

35 *omit* Br, conlei P₁CM, conlegi LRnS, concleah N
36 occidentali BrM, occidentalis P₁LC

populus fidelis masculini generis sexus intrat in ecclesiam, et alteram portam in sinistro latere per quam virgines et feminarum fidelium congregatio intrare solet.

Et sic in una basilica maxima populus grandis in ordine et gradibus et sexu et locis diuersis, interiectis inter se parietibus, diuerso ordine et uno animo omnipotentem orat dominatorem.

Et cum hostium antiquum portae sinistralis per quod sancta solebat Brigida in eclesiam intrare ab artificibus suis esset cardinibus situm totam concludere portam instauratam et nouam non potuit, quarta enim portae pars aperta sine conclusione et patefacta apparebat. Et si addita et iuncta ad altitudinem ostii quarta pars fuisset, tunc totam concludere portam posse altam et instauratam.

Et cum artifices alteram maius nouum facere ostium deliberarent quod totam concluderet portam aut tabulam facere iunctam in vetus hostium ut postea sufficere posset praedictus doctor et omnium praeuius artificum Hibernensium prudenti locutus est consilio: 'In hac superuentura nocte orare Dominum iuxta sanctam Brigidam fideliter debemus, ut ipsa nobis de mane quid in hoc opere acturi simus prouideat'.

Et sic orans iuxta monumentum Brigidae gloriosam noctem transegit, et de mane post ipsam surgens noctem oratione fideliter praemissa ostium antiquum trudens ac ponens in suo cardine, ianuam conclusit totam. Nec aliquid defuit de eius plenitudine nec ulla in eius magnitudine superflua pars reperta est.

Et sic illa Brigida illud extendit in altitudinem ostium ut tota porta illa sit ab eo conclusa nec in ea ullus locus patefactus videatur, nisi cum ostium retruditur, ut eclesia intretur. Et hoc virtutis Dominicae miraculum omnium oculis videntium illam ianuam et valuam manifeste patet.

Et quis sermonem explicare potest maximum decorem huius aeclesiae et innumera illius monasterii ciuitatis quam dicimus miracula, si fas est dici ciuitas, dum nullo murorum ambitu circumdatur. Conuenientibus tamen in ea populis innumerabilibus dum ciuitas de quo vita in se multorum nomen accepit, maxima haec ciuitas et metropolitana est, in cuius suburbanis, quae sancta certo limite designauit Brigida, nullus carnalis aduersarius nec concursus timetur hostium. Sed ciuitas est refugii tutissima deforis suburbanis in tota Scotorum terra cum suis omnibus fugitiuis, in qua thesauri seruantur regum et decorati culminis excellentissima esse videntur.

Et quis dinumerare potest diuersas turbas et innumerabiles populos de omnibus prouinciis[37] confluentes? Alii propter aepularum habundantiam, alii propter suas sanitates de suis languoribus, alii ad spectaculum turbarum, alii cum magnis donis et muneribus conuenientes ad solemnitatem natiuitates sanctae Brigidae, quae in die kalendarum februarii mensis dormiens secure sarcinam deiecit carnis, et agnum Dei in caelestibus mansionibus secuta est.[38]

EPILOGUE

Veniam peto a fratribus ac lectoribus haec legentibus immo emendantibus, qui causa obedientiae coactus, nulla praerogatiua scientiae suffultus pelagus inmensum virtutum beatae Brigidae et viris peritissimis formidandum, his paucis rustico sermone dictis virtutibus de maximis et innumerabilibus paruula intro cucurri.

Orate pro me Cogitoso nepote culpabili[39] Aedo[40] et ut audaciae meae indulgeatis atque orationem vestrarum clipeo Domino me commendetis exoro. Et Deus vos pacem euangelicam sectantes exaudiat. Amen.[41]

Explicit vita sanctae Brigidae virginis.[42]

37 *insert* hyberniae BrP₁CLM
38 *insert* cui est honor et gloria in saeculae saeculorum Br, *insert* facit eam permanere cui est honor et gloria in saeculae saeculorum amen explicit vita sancta brigidae virginis feliciter P₁
39 cogitoso nepote culpabili B, praecor ne imputetis me Br, cogitos ne inputeis CLRnS, cogitoso nepote culpabilis edoni N
40 *omit* BBrCLMRn
41 adiuuante domino nostro iesu christo qui viuit et regnat in secula saeculorum amen BrN
42 *omit* BBrN

The Vita Prima of Saint Brigid

1. There was a man of the nobility named Dubthach from the people of Leinster. He bought a slave woman named Broicsech who was beautiful, excellent in character and a good servant. Her master Dubthach desired her and slept with her so that she became pregnant by him. But when the wife of Dubthach discovered what had happened, she was very angry and said to her husband, 'Cast out this slave woman and sell her so that her child doesn't surpass my own children'.[1] But the man didn't wish to sell the slave woman, for he loved her very much and she was perfect in all her ways.

2. One day both the man and the slave woman were sitting in a chariot and went past the home of a certain druid. Hearing the sound of the chariot, the druid said to his slaves, 'See who is sitting in that chariot, for it sounds as though it is carrying a king'. Then the slaves said, 'We see no one except Dubthach in the chariot'. The druid said, 'Call him to me'.

When he was called, the druid said to him, 'The woman who is sitting behind you in the chariot, does she have a child in her womb?' Dubthach said, 'She does'. The druid said, 'Woman, by what man did you conceive?' She answered, 'By my master Dubthach'. The druid said to him, 'Take good care of this woman, for the child she has conceived is extraordinary'. Dubthach answered, 'My wife is trying to force me to sell this slave woman, for she fears her child'. The druid said, 'The children of your wife will serve the seed of the slave woman until the end of the age'. The druid then said to the slave woman, 'Be steadfast in your spirit, for no one will be able to harm you. The grace of your child will set you free. You will give birth to a famous daughter who will light up the world like the sun in the height of heaven'. Dubthach said, 'I give thanks to you because until now I have not had a daughter, only sons'.

Dubthach and his slave woman then returned to his house. Truly he loved the slave woman all the more after the words of the druid.

---

1 Gen 21:10. Abraham's wife Sarah demanded that he expel her slave woman Hagar after he had fathered a child with her.

But his wife along with her brothers urged Dubthach again to sell the slave woman in a distant region.

3. In those days, at the prompting of God, two holy bishops coming from Britain entered the house of Dubthach. One was called Mel and the other Melchu. And Mel said to the wife of Dubthach, 'Why are you sad? The child of your slave woman will surpass you and your offspring. Nonetheless, love the woman as you love your own sons, for your children will benefit greatly from her child'.

4. Since the wife persisted in her anger, a certain poet of the Uí Néill came, inspired by God, and bought the slave woman of Dubthach. But Dubthach did not sell the child that she had in her womb. The poet therefore went away with the slave woman to his home region. In the same night the poet entered into his house, a guest arrived there, a holy man, who prayed to God through the night. And he saw often during that night a ball of fire in the place where the slave woman was sleeping and in the morning he told the poet.

5. Then a certain druid came from the north to the house of the poet and he sold that slave woman and gave her to the druid.

6. One day the druid invited the king and queen to dinner, but the queen was near to giving birth. Then friends and servants of the king began to ask a certain prophet what hour would be best for the queen to deliver her child. And this druid said, 'If it is born tomorrow with the sun rising, it will have no equal in the world'. But the queen gave birth to a son before that hour.

In the morning as the sun was rising, the slave woman of the druid came to the house carrying a jar filled with milk fresh from the cow. And as she put one foot across the doorway and still had the other foot outside, she collapsed and sat down in the doorway, giving birth to a daughter.

This indeed is how the prophet had said the slave woman would give birth – neither in the house nor outside the house. Then the infant was washed in the warm milk her mother was carrying.

7. After this the druid went with the slave woman to the region of Connacht and lived there because the mother of the druid was from Connacht, though his father was from Munster.

One day the slave woman went outside to milk the cows and left her daughter sleeping alone in the house. Then the house seemed to be burning with flames and everyone ran to extinguish the fire. But when they came near, there was no sign of a fire. Instead they saw the young girl playing inside the house with a beautiful face and rosy cheeks. And everyone said, 'This girl is filled with the Holy Spirit'.

8. On another day the druid and slave woman, with others also present, were sitting in a certain place when suddenly they saw a cloth that was touching the head of the girl burst into a glowing flame. But when they quickly reached out their hands, they could no longer see the fire.

9. On another day while the druid was sleeping he saw two clerics clothed in white garments pouring oil on the head of the girl. They were performing the rite of baptism in the usual way. One of them said, 'Call this virgin Brigid'.

10. One night the druid was awake, as was his custom, studying the stars of the heavens. And throughout the night he saw a burning column of fire rising from the small house in which the slave woman was sleeping with her daughter. He called to himself another man who saw the same thing.

11. One day the voice of the infant was heard praying to God as she stretched her hands to heaven. A man spoke to her and she responded, 'This will be mine, this will be mine'.

Hearing this the druid said, 'This response the infant gave is a true prophecy because this will be her place forever'. This afterwards was fulfilled, for today the *parochia* of holy Brigid is great in those regions.

But when the inhabitants of that land heard this, they came together to the druid and said to him, 'You remain with us, but let the girl depart from us who foretold that our regions would be hers'. The druid answered, 'I will not be parted from my slave woman and her daughter, but instead I will leave your land'. Then the druid with all his household went to his homeland in the province of Munster where he had an inheritance from his father.

But the holy girl became nauseous eating the food of the druid and vomited it up every day. The druid observed this and considered carefully the cause of the nausea. He discovered it and said, 'I am unclean. But the girl is filled with the Holy Spirit. She cannot tolerate my food'.

He then selected a white cow and reserved it for the girl. A certain Christian woman, a devout virgin, milked the cow and then the girl would drink the milk of that cow and not vomit it up, for her stomach had been healed. And this Christian woman became the foster-mother of the girl.

When the holy girl grew up, she served in the house and whatever food her hand touched or her eyes saw would multiply.

12. After these things, the desire entered into the heart of the girl to return to her father. Knowing this, the druid sent messengers to him telling him to receive his daughter as a free person. Then her father rejoiced greatly and came to the house of the druid. He led his daughter from there and her Christian foster-mother followed.

13. When her foster-mother became sick, she sent holy Brigid and another girl with her to the house of a certain man to ask for a drink of beer for her sickness. But they received nothing from him and returned home. Then holy Brigid went down to a well and filled

her vessel with water that became the finest beer. And when her foster-mother tasted it, she rose up cured.

14. Not long after this a certain honoured guest came to her father's house. Her father arranged for a meal of cooked meat and gave five portions to his daughter to cook. Her father then went out, but his guest was sleeping in the house.

A hungry dog then came to the house and Brigid gave it one portion. The dog came a second time and she gave it another portion. The guest saw this but said nothing, for Brigid thought he was sleeping.

Later her father returned to the house and discovered five portions untouched. The guest told him what he had seen and they said to one another, 'We are unworthy to eat this meat. It is better that it be given to the poor instead'.

15. A certain religious widow who lived in a nearby settlement asked holy Brigid's father if she might accompany her to a synod that was gathered at the plain of the Liffey. She was permitted to go by her father, and so they set out.

Then a holy man at the synod who was sleeping saw a vision and arose saying, 'I saw Mary and a certain man standing with her who said to me, "This is holy Mary who lives among you."'

And just as the holy man finished saying these things to the synod, the widow arrived with holy Brigid. Then the holy man said, 'This is Mary whom I saw, for I clearly recognize her features'. Then everyone glorified her as a type of Mary.

16. After this holy Brigid went to visit her mother whom she had left with the druid mentioned earlier. But her mother at that time was far from the home of the druid, having twelve cows with her for making butter.

And after holy Brigid came to her mother, she distributed butter every day to the poor and to guests, dividing the butter into twelve parts as if for the twelve apostles. One part would be larger as though for Christ, for she said, 'Every guest is Christ'.

17. On another day the druid and his wife came having a large vessel to fill with butter. But holy Brigid seeing the large vessel turned red in her face with shame, for she only had enough butter for one day and half of another.

When they had entered the house, the virgin served them with a cheerful spirit, washing their feet, putting food before them and feeding them generously. After this she went into the storeroom and prayed to God, then brought out the small amount of butter she had.

When the druid's wife saw she scorned it and mocked her saying, 'You have given us only a trivial amount'. The virgin answering said, 'Fill the vessel with the butter you have'. Then by the power of God the large vessel was filled from this modest amount of butter.

When the druid saw this miracle he said to holy Brigid, 'Let this vessel full of mysterious butter be yours along with the twelve cows that you have milked'. Brigid said, 'Keep the cows. Release to me my mother instead as a free woman'. The druid said, 'Behold, I give you the butter and the cows and your mother freed'.

Then the druid believed in the Lord and was baptized. But holy Brigid gave everything to the poor that the druid had given her and returned with her mother to her father.

18. After these things Dubthach began to consider selling his daughter into slavery because she was stealing so many things, for everything she saw she secretly gave to the poor.

On a certain day he took her with him in his chariot to go to the king. And when they reached the hall of the king, Dubthach left his chariot with her and went to the king. And a pauper came to holy Brigid and she gave to him the royal sword of her father that the king had given to him.

Then Dubthach said to the king, 'Buy my daughter so that she can be your slave'. The king answered, 'For what reason are you selling her?' Dubthach said, 'Whatever things come into her hands she steals'. The king said, 'Let her come to us'.

Dubthach went out to her and said, 'Where is my sword?' She answered, 'I gave it to Christ'. Her father became so angry he wanted to kill the virgin. The king then said to her, 'Why did you give my sword, your father's, to the poor'? She replied, 'If my God were to ask for you yourself and my father, I would give you and everything you have to him, if I were able'.

Then the king said, 'This girl, as I see it, Dubthach, is a great concern for me to buy and greater for you to sell'. Then the king granted to the virgin another sword to give to her father. After this Dubthach happily returned home with his daughter.

19. Not long after this, a certain honourable man came to Dubthach to seek the hand of his daughter in marriage. This was pleasing to her father and brothers. But Brigid rejected him. When they began to pressure her greatly to marry the man, holy Brigid asked almighty God to place some deformity on her body so that men might stop seeking after her.

Then one of her eyes burst and liquified in her head. For she preferred to lose an eye rather than the eye of her soul and to love beauty of the soul more than that of the body.

When her father saw this he permitted her to be veiled. Then her eye was restored and she was healed when she took the veil as described below.

20. Then holy Brigid along with three other women went to the borders of the Uí Néill to the two holy bishops, Mel and Melchu. They were disciples of holy Patrick and lived in the settlements of Meath.

And they had a certain disciple named Mac Caille. This man said to Mel, 'Behold, there are holy virgins outside who wish to receive the veil of virginity from your hand'. Then he led the women before the bishop. While the bishop was examining them closely, there suddenly appeared a column of fire above Brigid that reached to the roof of the church where she was.

Then holy Bishop Mel put the veil over the head of holy Brigid. And when the prayers had been said, Brigid, with her head bowed, touched the wooden foot of the altar with her hand. And from that hour the foot of the altar has remained fresh without any decay or blemish forever. And the eye of holy Brigid was immediately healed when she accepted the veil.

Eight other virgins received the veil at the same time as holy Brigid. And the virgins along with their parents said, 'Do not leave us, but remain with us and accept this region as your home'. Then holy Brigid stayed with them.

21. One day three religious men who were pilgrims came to Brigid along with her nuns and she fed them loaves of bread and cooked bacon. The men ate the bread but hid away the three portions of bacon not wishing to eat it.

On the next day Brigid greeted them and said, 'Look and see how much bread you have left'. When they looked they saw along with three portions of bacon three loaves of bread as well.

22. On another day two of these three men went out to do necessary work, but the third and youngest remained behind. When holy Brigid saw this she said to him, 'Why didn't you go out with your brothers to work?' He answered, 'Because I don't have the use of one hand and am not able to work'. When Brigid saw his defective hand, she healed it and immediately he went out to work with his companions.

23. When the day of Easter was drawing near, holy Brigid wished to have a banquet for all the churches that were around her in neighbouring settlements of Meath. But she didn't have provisions

for a banquet except for one vat of beer, for there was a shortage of food at those times in that region.

She put the beer from that vat into two basins, for she had no other vessels. And the beer was divided up and carried by Brigid to the eighteen churches that were around her. And there was enough for all of them for Holy Thursday and for Easter Sunday and for the seven days following Easter.

On that same Easter, a certain leper covered with leprosy came to holy Brigid and asked for a cow. Since she didn't have a cow she said to him, 'Would you like us to ask God to heal you of your leprosy?' He answered, 'That for me would be better than all gifts'.

Then the holy virgin blessed water and sprinkled it on the body of the leper and he was healed. Giving thanks to God, he stayed with Brigid until his death.

24. On another day, when one of the nuns of holy Brigid was sorely ill and suffering greatly, she asked for a little bit of warm milk, but they had no cow with them. Hearing this holy Brigid said to another nun, 'Fill a saucer with cold water and give it to the sick woman to drink'. And when she had done this, the vessel was filled with warm milk as if it had been milked that same hour. And when she drank it, she was healed.

25. Two virgins from the family of holy Brigid who were paralyzed and lived near her sent word to Brigid to come and heal them. Then holy Brigid went to them and blessed salt and water for them. The women took it and were healed. And they followed holy Brigid to her place.

26. After this two blind Britons, along with a leprous helper who served as a guide for both of them, came to holy Brigid and stood outside the door of the church where she was, seeking for her to heal them. And she sent word to them saying, 'Stay here a short while and go into the guest house and eat, then we will pray for your health'.

But they were indignant and said, 'You heal members of your family, but you neglect to cure us for Christ because we are strangers'. Accepting the rebuke, she went out from the church to them carrying holy water with her and sprinkled it on them. Then the leper was cleansed and the blind men given sight, praising God and giving thanks to her.

27. On another day a certain woman came along with her daughter bringing a cow as a gift for Brigid. But the cow's calf remained behind wandering in very dense woods and they were not able to move the cow without her calf.

Then with one voice they cried out saying, 'O Brigid, help us!' And immediately the cow became quiet and calm of mind and straightaway went to Brigid. Then she said to them, 'Don't worry about the calf. It will come after its mother following her footsteps'. And this is what happened.

28. On another day, after the seven days following Easter were completed, holy Brigid said to her nuns, 'Is the beer we prepared for the solemnity of Easter running low? I'm worried about our bishop Mel and the guests of Christ'.

The nuns answered saying, 'God will provide'. As soon as they had finished saying this, there came into the house two nuns carrying a jar full of water on their shoulders and they gave the jar to Brigid so that she might bless it in the usual way. But Brigid thought there was beer in the jar and said, 'We give thanks to God who gave us this beer for our bishop'.

And so it happened that the water immediately was changed into beer like the finest wine.

29. At this same time holy Brigid was suffering pain in the eyes and a terrible headache. Hearing about this, Bishop Mel sent to Brigid to come to him so that they might both go to seek out a doctor to cure her.

Brigid said, 'I don't want to seek out a doctor of the body, but nonetheless I will do what you wish'. And it happened that while the bishop and Brigid were on their journey seeking a doctor, holy Brigid fell from her chariot in the ford of a certain river and her head was wounded on a rock with blood gushing out. And by that blood mixed with water two women were healed and their tongues loosened.

It happened that after this the doctor they were seeking met them on the road. When he had touched the head of the virgin with his hand he said, 'O virgin, a doctor much greater than me has touched your head. For there was no better spot from which to shed blood. Always seek the doctor who is able to drive the sickness from you'.

Then the bishop said to her, 'Never again will I urge you to seek a doctor of the body'.

30. After these things the Bishops Mel and Melchu went out with holy Brigid to Mag Tethbae because there the bishops had a large monastery.

And while the holy woman with the holy men was staying there, one day the king of Tethbae was not far away from them at a feast. And when a certain peasant was lifting from the table of the king a vessel of marvellous craftsmanship and precious material – this vessel was called a sevenfold cup among those in the past – it fell from the hand of the peasant and broke.

The king was furious and ordered the man to be bound in chains for execution. Hearing this Bishop Mel went to plead for the poor man, but the king did not release him. Then Mel, carrying with him the fragments of the broken cup, came to holy Brigid. And she asked God and the cup was restored and given to the king and the poor man was freed. And the fame of holy Brigid filled that region.

31. There was in that region a certain holy and noble virgin, also named Brigid, who sent to holy Brigid so that she might come to

her house. Then Brigid went to her house, and that woman welcomed holy Brigid with great joy and washed her feet. And because of her footbath a certain virgin was healed who was lying sick in that house and she immediately rose up and served with the others.[2]

And when the food was set before them, holy Brigid began to look intently at the table. Then the holy virgin Brigid who lived there said to holy Brigid, 'What are you looking at so intently?' Brigid answered, 'I'm looking at a demon sitting on our table'. And the other Brigid said, 'If it is possible, I wish to see him'. Brigid responded, 'It is not impossible, but first let your eyes be signed with the cross so that you are able to bear to see his face'.

When her eyes were signed, she saw the enemy with his hideous and dark form and huge head, with flame and smoke pouring from all his orifices. Then holy Brigid said to him, 'Speak to us, demon'. And that one answering said, 'O holy virgin Brigid, I could not speak to you nor disobey your commands because you do not disobey the commands of God and are kind to his poor and least honoured'.[3]

And Brigid said, 'Why did you come here?' The demon answered, 'I dwell with one of the virgins here and it is because of her laziness I have a place with her. And when that virgin came here to be blessed, here I remained'.

Then that virgin was called to them and Brigid signed her eyes and she saw the horrid monster and she was afraid and trembled. And holy Brigid said to her, 'Behold the one you have been accustomed to nourish for so many years'. And on that day the virgin was freed from the demon.

32. One day in Mag Tethbae a certain woman brought to holy Brigid a gift of apples. In that same hour before the woman went home, lepers came begging.

2   Mt 8:15.
3   Mt 25:40.

Then Brigid said, 'Divide these apples among them'. Hearing this, the woman seized her apples from Brigid saying, 'I brought these for you and your virgins, not for lepers'. This was displeasing to holy Brigid and she said, 'You are wrong in refusing to give alms. And so your trees will not bear fruit ever again'.[4]

And thus it was. Then that woman having left saw her orchard and could not find an apple in it, though in the hour that she had left it was full of apples. And it remained barren forever.

33. At another time holy Brigid was making a journey through Mag Tethbae in a chariot. Then she saw a certain husband with his wife and whole family struggling with many cattle and carrying heavy burdens in the burning sun and they were exhausted.

Then Brigid was compassionate towards them and gave them her chariot horses to carry the load. But she remained sitting by the road with her nuns. And Brigid said to them, 'Dig under the ground nearby so that water will gush forth. For others are coming who have food but are thirsty with nothing to drink'. Then they dug and a stream gushed forth.[5]

After a little while along the same road came a chieftain with a great crowd of foot and horse soldiers. And hearing what holy Brigid had done about the horses, he gave two untamed horses to her. But immediately they became tame as if they had always been under a chariot.

After this there came along the same road the disciples and household of holy Bishop Patrick. And they said to holy Brigid, 'We are struggling along the way. We have food but lack drink'. Then the companions of Brigid said, 'We have prepared for you a drink of water from a stream. Holy Brigid predicted that you would be here'.

Then everyone ate and drank together, giving thanks to God and glorifying Brigid.

4   Mt 21:19.
5   Ex 17:6.

34. One day two men who were lepers followed the holy woman as she was going with a large crowd and, as was her habit, she was kind to them. But the wretched men began to fight and hit one another. The hand of the one who struck his companion first could not be straightened again. The right hand of the other one also that was raised to hit back could not be bent to his side again.

The hands of these wretched men therefore remained immobile until holy Brigid arrived.[6] Then those lepers repented and Brigid healed their hands.

35. And on another day the chariot of holy Brigid was borrowed to carry a sick man who was breathing his last on the final boundary of life. And when the sick man was carried in the chariot of holy Brigid, they came towards evening to the place where holy Brigid was. And during that night the sick man was better.

And on the next day with her blessing him he walked normally, with her helping. Then lepers came asking for the chariot and it was given to them with horses.

36. Holy Brigid, invited to another church in the region of Tethbae, went there to celebrate the day of Easter. But the abbess of that church said to her nuns on the feast of the Lord, 'Who from you today will wash the feet of our old and sick women?' And all of the young women, not wishing to do so, made excuses.

Then Brigid said, 'I will wash the poor and sick women'. Now there were in one home four sick women: the first a paralytic who lay immobile, the second fully possessed by a demon, the third blind, and the fourth a leper. Then Brigid began first to wash the paralytic. And she said, 'O holy Brigid, ask Christ that he might heal me'. And Brigid prayed and immediately she was healed and also the leper was cleansed and the demented woman was made well.

6   1 Kgs 13:4–6.

37. Holy Brigid was also invited by another church in the same region to spend a few days there. But by chance it happened that the whole household of the church went out and Brigid remained alone with a mute and paralyzed boy. But she didn't know that he was mute and paralyzed.

And in that same hour some lay people came seeking food. And Brigid said to the boy lying there, 'Do you know where the key to the kitchen is?' He said, 'I know'. Brigid said, 'Get up and give it to me'. And he rose up and gave the key to her and he served food to those guests with her.

The household returned and marvelled that the boy was speaking and walking, so he told how he had been healed. Then everyone gave thanks to God.

38. Then the holy Bishops Mel and Melchu said to holy Brigid, 'Do you want to go with us to Mag Breg to visit holy Bishop Patrick?' Brigid answering said, 'I wish to speak to him so that he might bless me'.

Then the bishops and holy Brigid went on their way. But a certain cleric having a large household and cows and carts and much baggage asked whether he might go with them to Mag Breg. But the bishops refused in case he make them late because of the multitude of animals and baggage. And Brigid said to them, 'Go on before us. For I will remain and help them'. Then she remained behind.

She said to the household, 'Why don't you put the baggage in carts'? They said, 'Because our paralyzed brother and blind sister are lying sick in the carts'. Then with night coming they ate and drank. But Brigid alone fasted and stayed awake. In the morning she poured morning dew on the feet of the paralytic and immediately he rose up healed and the blind woman regained her sight. Then they put the baggage in the carts and continued on their journey giving thanks to God.

And while they were walking on the road, they saw a certain farmer by himself who by great labour was milking cows. Brigid said, 'Ask him why he's working alone without help'. He said, 'Because my whole family is ill. In one house lie twelve sick people'. Then Brigid told her nuns to milk the cows with him. Then the farmer asked that they accept a meal for their labour. They accepted and ate next to the bank of a certain river, except for Brigid who fasted. Then holy Brigid blessed water and sprinkled it on the house of the farmer and healed all the sick who were in it.

39. From there they went straightaway to a place called Tailtiu. There the holy bishop with many other bishops was sitting in an assembly. And in that council there was a great discussion. A certain virgin who had fallen into sin said that the infant she had born was by a certain bishop from among the disciples of holy Patrick named Brón. But he denied it.

Then everyone who was in the council, hearing of the marvellous deeds of holy Brigid, said that this question could be settled by her. Therefore the woman was led with her infant in her arms to Brigid outside the council.

Brigid said to her, 'By whom did you conceive this infant?' She answered, 'By Bishop Brón'. Brigid said, 'I don't think so'. Then Brigid bowing herself to holy Patrick said, 'Father, this question is for you to settle'. Patrick answering said, 'My dear daughter holy Brigid, please reveal the truth'.

Thus holy Brigid made the sign of the cross on the mouth of the woman and immediately her whole head with her tongue swelled up, but even then she did not repent. Then Brigid blessed the tongue of the infant saying to him, 'Who is your father?' He responded, 'Bishop Brón is not my father, but someone who sits at the far end of the council, a despicable and vile man'.

Then everyone gave thanks to God and glorified holy Brigid. And the woman repented.

40. Then as evening fell everyone went here and there to their homes. But Brigid with her nuns went to the water.

Then a certain farmer invited her saying, 'I have a new house. I would like for you to enter it first with your nuns to consecrate it'. Brigid went out with him and he served her with great joy, for he had seen the miracle that Brigid had done that day in the council and served them food.

Then Brigid said to her nuns, 'The Lord has shown to me that this man is a pagan'. One of her companions answered saying, 'What you say is true, for this man more than all others greatly resisted holy Patrick and his disciples and refused to be baptized'.

Then Brigid said to him, 'We are not able to eat your food unless first you are baptized'. Then, moved by God, he believed with his whole house and was baptized by Bishop Brón, the disciple of Patrick.

On the following day Patrick said to Brigid, 'From this day it is not allowed to you to travel without a priest. Let your charioteer always be a priest'. And he ordained a priest by the name of Nathfroích, and he was the charioteer of Brigid his whole life.

41. In those days a certain layman came to holy Brigid carrying his paralyzed mother on his shoulders. When he arrived at the place where Brigid was in her chariot, he lay his mother down in the shadow of holy Brigid. And when that woman touched her shadow, she rose up saying, 'I give thanks to God because when I touched your shadow, O holy one of God, I was healed immediately and felt no pain'.[7]

In the meantime certain men came to holy Brigid bringing a demon-possessed man bound in chains. When this man realized that he was being led to Brigid, he fell to the ground saying, 'You will not carry me to Brigid!' And they said to him, 'Surely you can't know the place where Brigid stays?' He answered, 'I know and I knew it right away and I will not go to that place'. And he told

7 Acts 5:15.

them the exact name of the place where Brigid was and they were not able to move him from the ground.

Then they talked together and some of them went to holy Brigid and asked her to come to the man. And Brigid came with them. And when the demon saw Brigid coming to him from far away, he fled from the man. Truly whenever demons saw holy Brigid coming to them from anywhere, they were terrified and fled. And the man was made well and gave thanks to God.

42. At this time holy Brigid was staying at the church of holy Laisre. On a certain day towards evening holy Patrick came with a large crowd to stay at that church.

The community at the church was worried and said to Brigid, 'What should we do? We don't have enough food for such a large crowd'. Holy Brigid said to them, 'How much do you have?' They said to her, 'We don't have anything except twelve loaves and a small amount of milk and one egg that we cooked for you and your nuns'. And Brigid said, 'That will be enough for all of us, for sacred scripture will be read to us so that we will forget about bodily food'.

From that small amount of food both groups of Patrick and Brigid ate together and were filled. And they sent back a greater amount than the food that holy Laisre had offered before.[8] And afterwards holy Laisre offered herself and her place to holy Brigid forever.

43. In the same place when holy Brigid was a guest there, a certain husband came asking that holy Brigid bless water for him that he could sprinkle on his wife. For the wife hated her husband. Then Brigid blessed water and the home was sprinkled with water along with the food and the drink and the bed, all while the wife was away. And from that day the wife loved her husband with love beyond measure as long as she lived.

---

8   Mt 15:32–9; Mk 6:31–4; Lk 9:12–17; Jn 6:1–14.

44. In those days there came to holy Brigid a certain virgin of God from the Uí Meic Uais seeking alms from every house. Brigid said to her, 'You will have my cloak or a cow that someone gave to me'. And the woman said, 'It would be no use to me to receive those things. For thieves will come along the way and take them from me'. And Brigid said, 'You will have my belt. For you told me there were many sick people in your region and by my belt dipped in water in the name of Jesus Christ you will heal them and they will give you food and clothing'.

And so she took the belt and the first person she went to was a sick boy whom his parents loved and she healed him and she was given good clothing. Thus she continued all the years of her life. For she healed every sickness and received many riches. And from these riches she bought many fields and became wealthy and gave to the poor.

45. The day before a certain solemnity, one of her disciples whom Brigid had fostered came to holy Brigid at Cella Roboris[9] bringing her alms. And when she had presented the gift, she said, 'I will return to my home so that my parents may come to pray with you through the night. But I will remain there to guard the house and cattle'. Brigid said, 'Not so, but you remain here and let your parents come. The Lord will preserve your property and home'. And thus her parents came as she said and they all celebrated the feast with holy Brigid.

But in the middle of the night thieves came to their house knowing the residents had gone to visit the holy woman and they stole the cattle. And when they came to the River Liffey, they found the river flooding and were not able to drive the cattle across the river.

And when they had laboured the greater part of the night, they made a plan and tied all their clothing above the heads of the cattle and their weapons as well. Then halfway across the river the cattle

9 Kildare (Latin *Cella Roboris*, Irish *Cell Dara*).

turned back carrying the spoils and weapons of their enemies above their heads and ran across the plain of the Liffey with the naked men chasing behind them. The cattle did not go back to their own home but went directly to the settlement of Brigid. At first light they arrived and everyone recognized the cattle and thieves.

Then the thieves gave praise to God and repented before holy Brigid in her settlement. As for the farmer, he went home rejoicing with his cattle and gave thanks to God.

46. Another girl, on the day before a certain feast, came with similar alms to holy Brigid. When she had accepted her gift the girl said, 'I will go back to my home because I didn't leave anyone there except for my foster-father who is very old and paralyzed and not able to milk cows or guard the house'. Holy Brigid said, 'Remain here tonight and let your cows be unmilked. God will guard your home'.

Then she stayed and on the next day, having received the Eucharist, she returned and found the cows and calves feeding happily and without distress in separate fields. And she saw the old man who had not yet seen night nor slept nor sensed the passing of time, as if in that same hour the girl had left him. And then the girl gave thanks to God and glorified Brigid.

47. At that time holy Brigid made a grand dinner in honour of the solemnity of the Lord, but this dinner was divided among the poor. Her community was quite upset about this. And the people, as was the custom, came to the feast day.

Now in that region a certain very wealthy farmer was bringing a banquet for his king in a wagon on the same feast day. That man became lost on the roads and a cloud covered him and he could not recognize the road he had known before until straightaway he came to the door of the church of holy Brigid.

Knowing this, holy Brigid went out to meet him and asked where he was going. He was moved by God to give all his things to holy Brigid saying, 'For this reason the Lord made me lost in my own land. Truly I shall make another banquet for the king'.

When the king heard about this he gave this farmer with all of his people to serve Brigid forever. The same king also sent another wagon full of food as supplies for the solemnity to holy Brigid. With this food the huge gathering of the whole people was fully satisfied.

48. A certain queen came to holy Brigid with good gifts among which was a skillfully-made silver chain that had a human figure at the end. The nuns took this chain and hid it in their treasury. But Brigid shared everything else with the poor.

One day a certain poor man came to Brigid and she, having nothing to give, went out to the treasury of the nuns and found there the previously-mentioned chain and gave it to the poor man. The nuns discovering this said to Brigid, 'Because of you we have lost all the things that God sent to us, for you give everything to the poor and leave us destitute'.

Then Brigid said to them, 'Go right away and look for the chain where I usually pray in the church. Perhaps you'll find it there'. And when they looked they discovered there a chain of the same sort and brought it to Brigid. Then Brigid said to them, 'Didn't I tell you, "Look for it"?' And the nuns kept this chain with them always as a testimony of the miracle and never sold it.

49. Cellan, a holy bishop and prophet of God who lived on the right side of the plain of the Liffey, came in a chariot to holy Brigid and stayed with her for a few days.

On a certain day wishing to return to his own place, he said to Brigid, 'Bless with care my chariot'. And she blessed it. The charioteer of that bishop, however, hitching the chariot had forgotten to put the linchpins on the wheels. Then the chariot and the bishop went swiftly across the plain.

And when, after a great portion of the day had passed, the bishop looked at the chariot and saw he had no linchpins. Then he jumped out of the chariot and fell on the ground and gave thanks to God and blessed holy Brigid, remembering her blessing.

50. One day holy Brigid came through the plain of the Liffey, and another holy virgin was with her sitting in one chariot. The charioteer was preaching to them the word of God. And Brigid said to him, 'Don't turn your face from us when you preach the word of God. Put your reins behind you. For our horses will go on the right path to our home'.

And thus it was. The horses went on a straight path through the plain. And while the charioteer was preaching diligently to the virgins and they were listening with intent ears and a curious spirit, one horse slipped its head and neck from the yoke and was walking unharnessed behind the chariot with no one noticing.

But a certain king was sitting near the road on a high place and he said in amazement to those sitting around him, 'Brigid sits praying in that chariot not noticing the horses. The Lord alone fills her mind'. Then the horse hearing the noise of the admiring crowd came up to the chariot and put its neck back under the yoke by itself. Then the shouting of the king and the people went up and the amazing miracle was told throughout the whole region and they glorified God and Brigid.

51. A certain leper of the Uí Néill came to Brigid seeking a cow from her. She said to the herdsman, 'Give a cow to him'. And the herdsman asked, 'Which cow shall I give to him?' Brigid said, 'Give him the best cow and the best calf'.

Then they picked out the best of the calves and letting it go the best of the cows ran to it lowing and the two were so fond of each other that scarcely could anyone separate them. But that cow whose calf had been taken away loved the calf of the other cow as if it were her own.

The leper said to Brigid, 'I am not able alone to drive the cow to my province'. Brigid said to her charioteer, 'Go with the leper'. It happened that at that hour the charioteer was cooking meat in a cauldron. The charioteer said, 'Who will cook this meat?' Brigid said, 'You yourself will come back to it quickly'.

And it was done just as she said. For the charioteer went with the leper on a journey of two days in an instant and in that same instant immediately returned and found the meat in the cauldron not yet cooked. And everyone marvelled that the charioteer was able to travel a journey of two days in a single instant. But God granted the wish of holy Brigid.

52. There was a shortage of bread in the plain of the Liffey at another time. Brigid was asked by her community to seek out grain and to go to Mag Géisille to holy Bishop Ibor to seek food from him. Brigid agreed to the wishes of those asking and went out on the journey.

Holy Ibor rejoiced with a great joy at the arrival of holy Brigid, but he did not have food for guests except dry bread and bacon. Then Bishop Ibor and holy Brigid ate the bread and bacon in the time of the forty days before Easter.

Two virgins among the companions of Brigid did not eat their portions and those parts were turned into two serpents. When this was told to Brigid, she reprimanded those virgins severely in front of Ibor and ordered them to remain outside and fast with tears. And Brigid said, 'Let us fast with them and pray to God'. And thus they did. And those two serpents were changed into two hosts of the purest and whitest bread. And one host was given to Bishop Ibor and the other to holy Brigid. And they were hosts for the Eucharist on Easter and the birthday of the Lord.

And Bishop Ibor said to holy Brigid, 'For what reason did you come here during Lent?' Brigid answered, 'So that I might ask you for a year's supply of bread'. Then Ibor smiled and said, 'O Brigid, if only you could see and know how little food we have. You won't be able to take even a small measure of grain with you'. Brigid said, 'I don't think this is so, for there are twenty-four wagon-loads in your granary'.

And thus by the will of God, the small amount that Ibor had increased and twenty-four wagon-loads were discovered in the granary just as Brigid said. And they divided them between themselves. Twelve wagon-loads were for Ibor while Brigid, with twelve wagon-loads, returned to her home.

53. A certain king came to Brigid to celebrate the solemnity of Pentecost. And when he had celebrated there that night, he rose up very early at daybreak to go to his home. They sped away quickly in chariots and on horseback. But holy Brigid, after finishing the solemn ceremonies of the day, went to the table and a large meal was served to all.

But Lommán, a very arrogant leper inspired by the devil, refused the food of holy Brigid, as usual, unless Brigid gave him the spear of the king mentioned before who earlier in the morning had set out towards his home. Everyone said to the leper, 'You saw the spear yesterday. Why didn't you immediately ask for it to be given to you?' That one said, 'Because only today did I begin to desire it'.

Then holy Brigid and everyone else asked him to eat, but they did not prevail. Brigid also refused to eat food until the prideful leper ate. Then Brigid sent horses after the king to request from him the spear. They rushed off and then crossing one mountain, they discovered that king at the ford of a certain river and made their request. The king was agreeable and gave them the spear saying, 'If holy Brigid had asked for all my weapons, she would have received them immediately'.

Then the horsemen sent by Brigid asked, 'Where did the king delay from the beginning of the day until the ninth hour?' His companions with him said, 'We did not delay but always at great speed made our journey. We indeed know that holy Brigid by the will of God restrained us so that the pressing request of the leper might be resolved quickly'.

Then everyone praised the Lord and Brigid. And the king went on his way quickly, not as before. And the men sent out returned swiftly to Brigid with the spear of the king and for that she gave thanks to God.

54. When Brigid was in a certain church and while she was sitting next to the door of that place, she saw a man walking in the valley by the bank of a river bent under a heavy burden. Taking pity on him she said to her nuns, 'Let us go to the man and carry the burden on his way with him'.

Brigid then said to him, 'Give to us the burden that weighs you down and is making you so bent over'. Answering he said to her, 'No burden weighs me down but an old ailment that I've had since my youth'. That man asked the name of the virgin and it was told to him that it was Brigid. He said, 'I give thanks to God because I've found the one I've been seeking for a long time. I wish for you to fast for a night and a day and ask God to straighten my body'. And Brigid said to him, 'Come to the guest house and rest in it this night and I will do what you wish'.

Then holy Brigid during that night fasted and prayed to God for him. When morning came she went to the guest house and said to the bent man, 'Go to the water of the river and wash yourself in the name of the Saviour and pray to God, then straighten your neck and do not go down until I tell you to'. And as that one said thus he did and was healed and gave thanks to God who straightened his body bent after sixteen years.[10]

55. After these things holy Brigid went with holy Bishop Patrick to the northern part of Ireland.

On a certain day holy Patrick was preaching the word of God to his people, but at that hour holy Brigid was asleep. And after she woke up, Patrick said to her, 'O Brigid, why were you not awake for the word of Christ?' When she had heard these words, she bowed down seeking pardon saying, 'Forgive me, father. Forgive me, holy lord. For in that hour I saw a dream'. And Patrick said, 'Describe it

10 Lk 13:13.

to us'. Brigid said, 'I your handmaid saw four ploughs ploughing this island and sowers sowing seed. And immediately it grew and began to mature and streams of new milk filled the furrows. And those sowers were dressed in white garments. After this I saw other ploughs and black ploughmen, who uprooted that good crop and tore it with the ploughs and sowed it with thorns and rivers of water filled the furrows'.

And Patrick said, 'O virgin, true and wonderous is the vision you saw. We are the good ploughmen who with the ploughs of the four evangelists tear open human hearts and we sow the word of God and we offer the milk of basic teaching. But truly in the end of the age evil teachers will come working with bad people who will subvert our teaching everywhere and lead astray almost everyone'.

56. On another day a certain leper came to holy Brigid asking if his clothes could be washed with water. And Brigid said to him, 'I will do what you ask'. And the leper said, 'I don't have any clothing except what will be washed'. And Brigid said to one of her nuns, 'Give your cloak to the leper until his clothes are washed'.

But that nun, not obeying, was struck with a disgusting stench and leprosy for the space of one hour. But another nun gave her own cloak to the leper. Then the leper, after he had taken off his clothes, was cleansed of his leprosy.

57. In that time after these things holy Brigid with her nuns acquired the site of a church in Mag Inis near the dwelling of Patrick. And afterwards during the season of Lent a shortage of bread threatened.

On a certain night eight men who were thieves came to steal the four horses that Brigid had with her. Then one of the virgins who was awake said to Brigid, 'Our horses are being taken away by theft'. Brigid said, 'I know, but do nothing. The ones who are taking them are more numerous and stronger than us'.

Then the thieves with the four stolen horses went to the house of a certain man living in a nearby place and went into the granary and found in it fifty measures of winnowed seed-corn. And they stole every single measure, carrying them on the four horses and on their shoulders and came to the dwelling place of the virgins, thinking that they had come to their own house. And they entered into the small hut, tied up the horses in a secluded corner and fell into a deep sleep after being awake so long.

When morning came, the men whose grain had been stolen came to the dwelling place of the virgins and said to Brigid, 'Thieves stole our grain and we tracked the footprints of the thieves and horses up to your door. We ask you not to conceal them'. Then holy Brigid went out to the thieves and woke them saying, 'Why did you bring the stolen goods to us?' And they said, 'Because we thought we'd come to our own home'.

Then holy Brigid sent for holy Bishop Patrick who was staying nearby. And Patrick came immediately to the men and the thieves were freed and repented. And the other men brought their own grain to Brigid along with her virgins, for they knew that it had been given to the virgins by God.

58. One day holy Patrick was preaching the word of God to the crowds and to holy Brigid. Then everyone saw a cloud of great brightness descending from the sky to the dark earth on a rainy day. And illuminated by a huge bolt of lightning it stood for a little space of time in a place nearby next to that crowd. And after these things it went away to Dún Lethglaisse where Patrick is buried. And the cloud stayed there a little while and then disappeared.

And the crowd did not dare to ask holy Patrick what this miraculous sign meant, but asked holy Brigid. And Brigid said, 'Ask Patrick'. Hearing this Patrick said, 'You and I both know. Reveal to them the mystery'. And Brigid said, 'That cloud, as I think, is the spirit of our holy father Patrick, which came to visit the places where his body will rest after his death and will be buried. For in a nearby place, for a little while, his body will rest and after this will be carried to be buried at Dún Lethglaisse. And there his body will remain until the day of judgment'.

Then Patrick told Brigid to make with her own hands a linen shroud and in that afterwards the body of holy Patrick was wrapped and remains in that place.

59. There was a certain nobleman, rich and good, in Mag Machae who had a very serious illness and ailment and was not able to be cured by any of the doctors. And he sent to holy Brigid so that she might come to him. And she went to his home.

When she had seen his home from far away, she stood and said, 'From whatever direction the wind blows, to that house that wind also carries with it a curse and disease to that man'. That man hearing this said, 'To no person have I done evil nor have I harmed either clerics or craftsmen'.

Then his herdsman said, 'I have heard everyone around you as in one voice cursing you because your farm manager while building fences changed all the level and straight roads into rough and crooked and thorny places'.

Hearing this holy Brigid said, 'This is the cause of your sorrows'. Then all the roads were changed back into level roads and all the travellers blessed him. And the man was healed and gave thanks to God and Brigid.

60. On a certain day holy Brigid was sitting beside the settlement of Machae with her nuns. She saw two men carrying with them a vessel full of water. And when they drew near, they asked the water be blessed by Brigid and she blessed the water and the men.

And while they were going away, it happened that the vessel fell to the ground on its side and it was not broken nor did the water pour out because Brigid had earlier blessed it. And holy Patrick ordered that the water be saved and divided among all the churches of the region so that it might be used for the Eucharist of the blood of Christ and so that the sick might be sprinkled with that water for healing. And thus it was done. And they praised God through Brigid.

61. And holy Brigid sent to holy Patrick so that he might preach the word of God to her while he with his disciples and she with her nuns were gathered together in one place. And for three days and nights Patrick did not cease to speak nor did the sun set on them, but everyone thought it was but one hour.

But a certain man not knowing these things came from another place and said to holy Patrick, 'Why have you been sitting here such a long time?' Patrick asked, 'What hour of the day is it now?' That man said, 'For three days and nights you have remained here'. And Patrick said, 'For forty days and nights we would have been here unless someone from the outside had come to us and we wouldn't have felt any tiredness or hunger, thanks to the gift of divine grace'. Then everyone returned to their own homes.

62. After these things holy Brigid came to Mag Breg. And since holy Brigid was staying in another church, the wife of the son of King Conall came to her so that Brigid might pray to God for her because she was barren. And she brought with her a silver vial. But nonetheless holy Brigid did not come out of the church to greet her but sent a nun.

Then the nun said to Brigid, 'Why didn't you pray to the Lord for the queen that she have a son when you often pray for the wives of common people?' And Brigid said, 'Because the common people serve and they all call on the Father. But the sons of kings are serpents and sons of blood and sons of death, except for a few chosen by God. But nevertheless because the queen beseeches us, go and say to her that she will have offspring, but it will be a bloody and cursed stock, and for many years they will hold the kingdom'. And thus it was.

63. One day there came to holy Brigid a certain insane man who ran from place to place driven by madness who struck everyone

walking through that place. And holy Brigid said to him, 'Preach to me the word of the Lord Jesus Christ'.

The insane man said, 'O holy virgin Brigid, I will obey your commands. Love God and everyone will love you. Honour God and everyone will honour you. Fear God and everyone will fear you'.

And when he had said these things, he fled with a shout.

64. On that day Conall son of Niall came to holy Brigid walking on the road and said to her, 'O holy Brigid, bless me earnestly so that my brother Cairpre, who hates me, doesn't kill me'. And Brigid said to him, 'I will bless you. Let your household go ahead and we will follow them. For it isn't right for us to walk with them. You however remain'.

Then they went forward. And when everyone had gone up the hill, one of the nuns said to Brigid, 'Alas Brigid, what will we do? Behold Cairpre comes after us. And these two brothers will now kill each other'. And Brigid said, 'Our God will not do this to us'.

And when Cairpre had come he said, 'O holy Brigid, bless me, for I fear my brother Conall in these places'. Then the two brothers crossed over the hill together but did not recognize each other. God blinded their eyes so that they would not know each other on account of holy Brigid.

And Brigid blessed them and Conall and Cairpre kissed each other, not recognizing each other. And each went his own way and everyone magnified the name of God and of Brigid for this miracle.

65. At another time the same Conall came to holy Brigid with his followers wrapped around with evil signs. And he said to Brigid, 'We seek your blessing, for we wish to go into distant regions and loose these our bonds. For to undo them we need to murder and kill enemies'.

And Brigid said, 'I ask my almighty God that you put aside these signs of the devil as you wish and not be harmed by anyone and not hurt anyone'. And Christ quickly fulfilled this wish of the virgin.

For they went out into the region of the Cruthin and attacked there a certain fortress and burned it, as it seemed to them. And they thought they had killed and beheaded many people. And they returned to their native land with shouts and great jubilation and the heads of the enemies.

And when daylight had come, they did not see heads or blood nor was there any blood on their clothes or weapons. And they said to each other with confusion, 'What has happened to us? Where are the things we saw?' Then they sent messengers to the fortress they had burned down to ask if anything had happened to them. They said to the residents of that fortress, 'Has anything new happened to you?' And the residents said, 'No, except we found stalks burned this morning and the fortress damaged and large stones all around. But we saw no one nor do we know who did this'.

The messengers having returned reported these things to Conall. Then Conall with his companions laid aside their signs and did not come against God or Brigid. And this was pleasing to Brigid and she said to Conall, 'Because you put aside your signs for me, in any danger call on me. I will defend you and you will safely escape'.

And this promise was fulfilled, for at the beginning of the year Conall marched with his large army into the lands of enemies and there made a great slaughter and with a great triumph returned to his own country. And since he was tired he went into another fortress. Then his comrades said to Conall, 'If we remain in this place, our enemies will come and kill us'. And Conall said, 'I am tired. I will not leave from here. Holy Brigid promised that she would defend me in every danger. I believe that her promise is true. Into her hands I commend myself with my companions in this night'.

And right away in that night the enemies came after them. And when they came near to that fortress where Conall was, they sent four men to spy out the fortress. And they entered into that fortress and there saw a large group of clerics sitting in clerical clothing and a fire in the middle of them and books open in front of them. For the army had placed the heads they cut off so that each had one before him. And so the men seemed as if they were studying open books.

And the scouts returned telling of these things. And again they sent three other men, wiser ones, and they in the same way saw clerics with open books just as before. Then the army of the enemies returned to their own region and sent messengers, who announced these things to Conall, to bring back the heads. Then Conall gave thanks to God and Brigid.

66. At another time holy Brigid was asked to go out to a king who was in Mag Breg so that she might free another man who was arrested by the king. Brigid said to the king, 'Release to me the man you hold and I will give to you a reward for him'. The king responded, 'If you were to give me the whole of Mag Breg I would not free him, but instead I will kill him today'. And scarcely did Brigid obtain the man's life for one more night.

Then Brigid during that night in a nearby place sat with the relatives and friends of the arrested man and she was without sleep. Then the friends of the king said to him, 'Unless the arrested man is killed during this night, tomorrow he will not be able to be killed, for holy Brigid will free him. We have therefore determined a plan so that we seize him from your hands by force and then without your knowledge we kill him. And you will be blameless'.

But Brigid discovered this deceit. And so at the beginning of the night a dream appeared to the arrested man and he saw Brigid standing by him who said to him, 'Behold, evil men plan to kill you during this night. But when you are dragged away by them to be killed, call out my name repeatedly. And when the chain is removed from your neck so that you may be killed, turn to the right and you will find us immediately. We will wait for you'.

The man woke up and immediately they came and seized the arrested man from the hands of the king and loosed the chain to kill him. But when he was unshackled he turned towards Brigid. But they, as they thought, killed the man and cut off his head. On the next day however there was no head or blood to be seen. Then they all were dumbstruck with wonder. But when the sun had risen, Brigid sent to the king to release the arrested man to her. The king however hearing these things repented and set the arrested man free.

67. One day some hateful and vain men having diabolical signs on their heads came to Brigid seeking someone to kill. And they asked to be blessed by Brigid. And she asked them in return to lift a heavy burden by their labours.

And they said, 'We cannot put aside our signs unless someone holds them so they don't fall to the ground'. And she took them and marvelled at the shape of the signs and blessed them with the sign of the cross of Christ.

They went away on their journey seeking to shed blood. And they found a certain common man and killed him and cut off his head. The common man however went out safely to his home and they were seeking his body or head or blood and did not find them. And they said to each other, 'Because of holy Brigid we have killed and did not kill the man'. And this deed was made known throughout the whole region. And those men left behind their signs and glorifying God, magnified holy Brigid.

68. A certain king came with gifts into the plain of the Liffey to holy Brigid so that he might be blessed by her. And Brigid blessed him gladly. Then the king returned on his way. On the following night when the king was tired on the journey, he slept along with his companions and guards.

And there came a certain man who was an enemy of the king and entered into the fortress and into the house and holding a candle looked for the king and found him sleeping and his sword was next to him by his neck. Taking the sword, he stabbed him in the heart three times and immediately turned in flight. Then everyone, sensing the shedding of blood, rose up and made a great commotion thinking the king was dead.

But the king was in fact sleeping in a deep sleep and afterwards waking up consoled them. And after this, though slightly wounded, he remained in good health saying, 'By that blessing of holy Brigid, who blessed me today, she guarded me'.

On the next day with many gifts he returned to holy Brigid and she made peace between the king and his enemy who killed him and between their people forever, with God granting this through the merits of holy Brigid.

69. After this holy Brigid wished to go to the regions of the Munstermen travelling with Bishop Erc, a disciple of holy Patrick, because the family of Erc was of the Munstermen.

And when they had set out on the way, Brigid said to Bishop Erc, 'Show me, venerable father, under what part of the sky your family lives'. And when he had shown her, Brigid said to him, 'A war is raging now between one family and another family'. Erc said, I believe what you say is true, for when I came here from those regions, I left them quarrelling'. And Brigid said, 'Your family is now turned in flight'.

Then a youth of the household of Erc scoffed at her saying, 'How are you able to see a war over such a great distance of territory?' But Erc rebuked him lest he blaspheme the Holy Spirit.[11] And Erc said to Brigid, 'I ask of you, make a sign on the eyes of me and this boy so that we might see what you see'. Then she signed their eyes and they saw the war with their own eyes. Then the boy said to the bishop in a tearful voice, 'Alas, alas, my lord, now with my own eyes I see my two brothers by blood being beheaded!'

70. After this, along the road they chose, Brigid and the bishop went to Mount Ere and there in the middle of the journey they

11 Mt 12:31–2; Mk. 3:28–9; Lk 12:10.

struggled with hunger and thirst and were fatigued with great tiredness. And one of the boys said, 'A great mercy they would be showing if someone would give us help now'.

Brigid answered, 'With an eager heart I wish to give you all relief. If you wish to be filled with food and drink, wait here for the help of the Saviour. For I see a house in which gifts are being prepared for a certain church to be offered in the house of God. Thus it will come here in this hour. For behold, a meal has been prepared just now in packs'.

And while she was still speaking, those carrying the gifts arrived. And when they knew that Bishop Erc and holy Brigid had been sitting there and labouring in hunger, they were greatly pleased and gave to them the gifts saying, 'Accept these gifts that God has sent you. We do not have a better church than you'.

Then they gave thanks to God and ate there, but nevertheless they had nothing to drink. And Brigid said, 'Dig in the earth nearby'. And when they dug they found a clear spring, and that spring has flowed from that day till now under the name of Brigid. Then everyone glorified God and Brigid.

71. Then they came to Mag Femin and there was a large synod there, and for several days they stayed at the synod. And the bishop told the synod of the many miracles of Brigid.

At that time a terrible sickness was devastating the people and everyone asked Brigid to visit the sick. And the bishop said, 'The holy woman of God will not go to the places of illness, but bring your sick to her'. Then they brought to her the lame and the leprous and demon-possessed and everyone sick and, in the name of Jesus Christ, Brigid healed them all.

72. After these things holy Brigid went out to another man who was living alone as a solitary and was near the sea, not at all far from the place where Bishop Erc lived. And she remained there with her nuns for many years, as it is told.

Not far from them lived an anchorite who avoided looking at the faces of women, a man totally dedicated to God and perfect. Afterwards this anchorite wished to go to a certain island, and setting out on the road came near the place of Brigid. His companions thus said to him, 'Let us go to holy Brigid so that she might bless us'. The anchorite answered, 'You know my vow that I do not wish to see any woman'.

Then they rose up from their seats on which they had been sitting meanwhile and forgot all their baggage on the road and travelled a journey of a whole day. When evening had come they stayed in a certain guest house and then remembered their baggage and said, 'For this reason we lost our baggage, because we did not go aside to visit holy Brigid so that she could bless us'. And because of that fault they fasted that night.

When morning had come they returned to Brigid and discovered in her house their baggage. For Brigid had ordered her nuns saying, 'Go and bring back the baggage of the servants of God, which is on the road near us, so it isn't lost'. After they had come back to Brigid they passed three days and nights in praising God and in the preaching of the word of God.

Then the anchorite and his companions went out on the road and Brigid went with them. But Brigid seeing the heavy baggage had pity on them. At that same hour they saw two horses descending from the mountain towards them and they put their baggage on the horses. And when they had almost come to the end of their journey, Brigid said to them, 'Release the horses which you've had'. Then the horses fled and none of them knew from where or whose they were. Brigid returned to her house, but the anchorite went to his island.

But a certain layman arrived at that island with his wife and sons and daughters. The anchorite, while avoiding looking at the woman, asked the layman to leave the island, but he did not succeed. For the layman said that he held a field on that island inherited from his father. Then the anchorite sent to Brigid to come to him. And she came and while fasting asked the layman and did not succeed. On the next day however a huge eagle came and seized the infant of the wife of that layman. And the wife wailing and weeping came to Brigid. And Brigid said to her, 'Do not weep because the infant lives. Indeed the eagle placed it on a certain shore on the ground'. Then the wife went out and thus found the infant and came to Brigid and repented. The layman however remained hard and unrepentant and scolded his wife.

And when the layman was near the shore on the next day, suddenly a fierce wind came and carried him gently and smoothly across the sea to the nearest port. Then the layman with a contrite heart repented and vowed to God and Brigid that he would not enter the island again unless the anchorite permitted him to enter.

73. Also on another day religious guests came to holy Brigid, who was living in a place near the shore of the sea. Then Brigid said to a certain man from her household who was a fisherman and was accustomed to kill sea bulls, 'Go to the sea and if you are able, bring back something for the guests'.

Then he went and took his sea spear with him. Immediately a sea bull came to him and he threw his spear and fixed it in the bull. There were cords hanging from the head of the spear, but the cords were wrapped around the hand of the man. Then the gravely-wounded bull dragged the man with him in his boat through the sea. And the bull did not stop before it had arrived at the shore of Britain. Then the cord was cut on the rocks of the shore and the man remained in his boat by the shore. The bull however with the spear turned back into the sea and came straight back to the shore of that place where holy Brigid was and there the sea bull died.

And the man after a successful voyage in his boat arrived in the sixth hour and found the dead bull with the spear on the shore. And going home he told everyone about his voyage. Then everyone gave thanks to God and Brigid.

74. After these things holy Brigid came with her nuns to Mag Cliach and lived there in a certain place. Then a slave woman running away from her mistress came to Brigid. But her mistress followed her wishing to bring her back with her. Brigid asked the mistress to free the slave woman, but the mistress refused, for the slave woman wove many clothes.

Then that mistress grabbed the hand of her slave woman and dragged her by force from the side of Brigid and this was displeasing to Brigid. And when they had gone a short distance from holy Brigid, the right hand of the woman, which had grabbed the hand of the slave woman, withered. The mistress, seeing that she was not able to move her hand, wept and repented and sent the slave as a free woman to Brigid. And she herself was healed.

75. Holy Brigid was asked to go to a certain king in Mag Cliach to free a man who was in chains with the king. And Brigid went and entered into the house of the king and didn't find the king in his home, but friends of his were there, that is, the man who fostered him along with his wife and sons.

And Brigid saw harps in the house and said to them, 'Play your harps for us'. The friends of the king replied, 'There are no harpists in this house, but they have gone out on a journey'. Then another man who was with the companions of holy Brigid said jokingly to those friends, 'You play the harps yourselves and may holy Brigid bless your hands so that you may be able to do what she asks of you and obey her word'. And the friends of the king said, 'Let it be so. Let Brigid bless us'. Then they took up the harps and the unskilled harpists played.

Then the king returned to his house and heard the sound of music and said, 'Who plays this music?' Someone answered him, 'Your foster-father and foster-mother along with their sons, by the command of Brigid'. The king entered into the house and asked for a blessing from Brigid. And Brigid said, 'You in return release to me the bound man'. Then the king freely gave the bound man to her.

And the friends of the king were harpists until the day of their death and the descendants of them for many ages were greatly honoured by kings.

76. Two men who were lepers came to holy Brigid asking to be made well. Then holy Brigid prayed with fasting and blessed water for them and told them to wash each other in the holy water. And so it was done. And immediately one was healed and he was clothed in his washed garments.

And Brigid said to him, 'Wash also your companion'. He however seeing that he was clean and his clothes washed did not want to touch the leprosy of the other but gloried in his own health. But Brigid said to him, 'Because you wished for what he did for you, you ought to do similarly for him'. But he refused and spoke against her. Then Brigid herself got up and washed the leper and gave to him clean clothes.

The one who had been healed first said, 'I now feel there are sparks of fire on my shoulders'. And immediately his whole body was struck with leprosy because of his pride. But the other man was healed because of his humility and he gave thanks to God who healed him through the merits of holy Brigid.

77. One day holy Brigid with her virgins was walking in a plain and saw a certain young scholar running quickly. Brigid said to him, 'O young man, where are you running to so fast?' He answering said, 'I am running to the kingdom of God'. Brigid said to him, 'Oh that I might deserve to run with you to the kingdom of God. Pray for me that I may be worthy of it'. The scholar answered, 'You ask God that my path not be impeded and I in turn will ask that you and a thousand companions with you might go to the kingdom of God'. Then holy Brigid prayed to God for the young man and in those days he did penance and was devout to his death.

78. Two lepers came to Brigid seeking alms. She however having nothing that she could give to them, she gave to them the one cow

she had. One of them gave thanks, but the other was proud and ungrateful saying, 'Unless the cow is given to me alone, I will not take half of it'.

Then Brigid said to the humble leper, 'You wait a little while here with me and wait for what the Lord will send. And let the proud one alone take the cow as he says'. Then that one went out with the cow, but he was not able to drive it alone. Finally worn out by labour, he returned to Brigid and with many reproaches blamed holy Brigid saying, 'Because you did not give your cow gladly, I am not able to drive her alone. She is very difficult and untamed'.

Holy Brigid tried to console him but she was not able to calm him. And this was displeasing to holy Brigid and she said to him, 'You are a son of perdition! You will take the cow, but she will do you no good'.

79. On the same day a certain man came to Brigid with a cow as an offering and then the two lepers took their two cows and went out to a certain river. And that river pulled the proud leper with his cow into deep water and he was drowned and his body was never found. But the humble one escaped with his cow.

80. After these things holy Brigid came from Mag Cliach to the borders of Leinster to help the poor among her own relatives. And when she had come in a chariot through Mag Femin, she discovered there a certain man fencing a field. And the charioteer of Brigid said to him, 'Grant to us that holy Brigid may pass in a chariot through your field and afterwards you may put a fence around your field'. The man answered, 'No! Go around the field'. They tried to persuade him, but they didn't succeed.

Then Brigid said, 'Let us do as he says lest anything unpleasant happen because of this man'. But the charioteer drove the horses across the fence. Seeing this the man became furious and began to hit the noses of the horses with a club. And with the horses kicking, holy Brigid and the charioteer fell off the chariot, but were unharmed and the horses stayed in the same place.

Then Brigid said, 'Didn't I say to you to avoid this man? I saw that he was a man of pestilence and death'. Then that man continued his work making light of the evil he had done. And immediately he fell to the earth and died.

81. And so came holy Brigid to the outermost borders of the Leinstermen and entered into the province of the Uí Labratha and lived there in that place. Then a certain woman with a leprous daughter came to her so that she might be healed by her. Then Brigid fasting prayed and blessed water and ordered that the leprous daughter be sprinkled with that water. And immediately she was cleansed of her leprosy and gave thanks to God and to Brigid.

82. Certain religious men came to Brigid and preached the word of God. After this Brigid said to her cook, 'Prepare a meal for our excellent guests'. The cook answered saying, 'What meal will I give them?' And Brigid said, 'Give them bread and butter and onions and many dishes'. The cook answered, 'I will give them as you say, but first go to the church. For your cook has none of these things you're talking about!' And Brigid said to the cook, 'Sweep the floor of the kitchen and close it up and go to your home and pray in it. I will go to the church'.

On the sixth hour Brigid called the cook with a clap of her hands and said to her, 'It's time for our guests to be fed. Go to the kitchen and whatever you find in it, give them large portions'. Then opening the kitchen she discovered all the foods which Brigid mentioned and the food was not lacking for seven days and was enough for both the guests and the whole household of Brigid. And no one knew from where that food came or who had brought it except Brigid and her holy cook.

83. At another time a chorus of virgins came to holy Brigid having a question and said to her, 'Why in this place are there no water herbs of the kind holy people normally eat?'

For this reason on the following night holy Brigid prayed to God. And in the morning the nuns getting up saw the wells filled beyond measure with these herbs. And they were spreading over a large area and in those places they found a great multitude of these herbs which before were not seen in these places until Brigid asked – and almighty God gave to her as she asked.

84. With the fame of holy Brigid growing through many regions, certain religious men came with gifts to her from far away, and they carried these gifts to her in chariots and on horses. But by chance they came into dense woods. Night fell over them and not knowing the way they wandered in the woods and were not able to carry the chariots through the woods.

Then holy Brigid knew of their labour and prayed to God for them and said to her nuns, 'Kindle a fire and heat water for the guests'. Now that night was truly dark. Then the leaders of those men on foot saw a huge torch which went ahead of them on the way until they reached the house. Then Brigid went out to meet them and they gave thanks to God together and stayed there three days praising God.

After these things those men went back by the same route by which they had come on the previously mentioned night. And they saw the place was rough and uneven and they were not able to carry their chariots except on their shoulders and the horses they led by hand and went forward with the greatest labour because none of the experienced men knew there was a road in those places. But Christ on the earlier night had made that place level and clear on account of holy Brigid asking.

85. In a similar way, a certain bishop named Brón, whom we mentioned before, came with gifts to holy Brigid and with chariots and horses and with many companions. They came into dense woods and wandered about not knowing the way, just as we described happening previously. Then a wintery night fell over them.

But holy Brigid knowing this said to her nuns, 'Let us pray to God for our guests, because they labour coming to us, that God may have pity on their labours. I am about to tell you something extraordinary'.

Then those guests in the middle of the way suddenly saw Brigid's place, so they thought, and they saw Brigid rejoicing with her nuns coming along their way to greet them. She immediately led them into a great house, unhitched their chariots and horses, washed their feet and fed them an abundance of food. Then with the beds made, she put the guests to rest and Brigid and her nuns did everything for them that is necessary for guests, as they thought.

When morning came, Brigid said to her nuns, 'Let us prepare to meet our guests wandering so close to us, who have spent the night in the woods'. Then they hurried and found the guests sitting in the woods and with great happiness led them back to their home and carried out all the obligations of hospitality that had been shown to the guests in the night and together they gave thanks to God.

86. Holy Bishop Brón returned to his region and carried with him anointing oil from holy Brigid. Now he lived near the sea.

On a certain day the bishop was working on the shore of the sea along with a boy and put that anointing oil on a rock on the shore and the tide came in to its fullness. Then the boy remembered the anointing oil and wept. And the bishop said, 'Don't weep. For I believe that anointing oil of holy Brigid will not perish'. And so it was. For the anointing oil was on the dry rock and was not moved by the waves of the sea. And when the tide went out, they found it just where it had been put.

87. After this holy Brigid came to the home of her father Dubthach wishing after a long time to visit her parents. And her father rejoiced greatly at her arrival and asked her to stay in his house that night and she stayed.

During that night an angel came and woke Brigid and coming again woke her. The third time however he woke her more vigorously telling her, 'Quickly wake up your father and his household and your nuns, for enemies are drawing near wishing to kill your father with his household. But because of you God does not wish this. Get out quickly now – get out immediately – for this house now is about to burn!'

And when everyone was out, the enemy came right away and set fire to the house. Then her father said, 'O holy Brigid, your blessing guards us in this night from present death'. And Brigid said to him, 'Not only in this night, but until your old age blood will not be shed in your home'. And this has been fulfilled through many ages up till now. For when a certain man wished to strike down a certain virgin, his right hand that he reached out went rigid and his hand was not able to be withdrawn until he let go of the virgin.

But on the next day one of her nuns said to holy Brigid, 'Does an angel always help you as happened last night?' And Brigid said to her, 'Not only that night, but through all my life I have his help in everything. For every day he brings me happiness, for through him I daily hear the sounds of the heavens and spiritual songs of instruments. Also through him I hear the Masses that they celebrate to the Lord in distant lands as if they were near. And he offers my prayers day and night to God and whether present or absent he always hears me. Now by two examples I will show this to you.

'One time a certain leprous and ill woman asked me to bring her water and in pity take care of her other needs. So I blessed a vessel of water and gave it to her saying, "Put that between you and the wall so that no one touches it until I return". Indeed the angel blessed that water in my absence and it was changed into whatever taste the woman wished. For when she desired honey, it had the taste of honey. In the same way whenever she wanted wine or beer or milk or other drinks the same water was turned into those tastes by the wish of the sick woman.

'Again when I was a young girl, I made a stone altar in a girlish game and the angel of the Lord came and made holes in the four corners and put under it four stone feet.

'These two examples, O child, I have shown to you so that you might glorify our Lord'.

88. At the same time her father asked holy Brigid to go to the king of the Leinstermen to ask the king to give him the sword permanently that he had given for a time. And so holy Brigid went out to the king on the plain of the Liffey.

And when she was seated at the gate of his settlement, one of the king's slaves came to her saying, 'If you free me from the yoke of that king, I will be your servant forever along with my people and I and my family will become Christians'. Brigid said to him, 'I will ask for you'.

Then Brigid was called to the king. And the king said to her, 'O Brigid, what do you want from me?' She said to him, 'I ask that your sword be given to my father and one of your slaves released to me'. The king said, 'What will you give to me in exchange for these two great petitions?' Brigid said, 'If you wish, eternal life I will give to you and also that your descendants will rule through the ages'. The king said, 'A life that I cannot see I do not seek. Concerning sons who will come after me, I don't care. But give me two other things: that long may I live in this present life which I love and that in every place and in every war I be victorious. For we have a perpetual battle against the Uí Néill'. Brigid said to him, 'These two things will be given to you: long life and victory in every war'.

Not long after these things he went out with a few men into Mag Breg. And when he saw the multitude of the enemy, he said to his own men, 'Call on Brigid for help so that the holy woman fulfils her promises'. And they cried out to the heavens. Then immediately the king saw holy Brigid go forth before them into battle with her staff in her right hand and a column of fire was burning from her head to the sky. Then the enemy turned in flight. And the king and his household gave thanks to God and to Brigid

After this that king waged thirty wars and won them all, led nine successful campaigns against Britain and received tribute from many kings so that he would fight with them since he was unbeatable.

89. It happened after the death of that king that the Uí Néill came to destroy the Leinstermen. Then the Leinstermen came upon a good plan saying, 'Let us put the dead body of our king between us in the chariot and let us fight around his corpse against the enemy'. And thus they did. Then the Uí Néill turned in flight. For the divine gift given through holy Brigid remained in the king and thus it was even after the death of that king.

90. On another day a certain holy man came to the home in which Brigid was praying alone and found her standing and stretching her arms in prayer to the sky. And he neither heard nor saw anything else. At the same hour a great clamour by the inhabitants of that place sounded, for at that hour the calves rushed to the cows. But this holy woman did not hear, her mind being apart and intent on God.

Then that man left her in that hour so as not to disturb her prayer. But in another hour he returned to her and said to her, 'O holy one of God, why did you not run to the shouting of the people?' She said, 'I did not hear this clamour'. That man said to her, 'What other thing did you hear?' Brigid answered, 'In the city near the tombs of holy Peter and Paul I heard Masses, and I very much desire the order of this Mass and universal rule to be brought to me'.

Then Brigid sent wise men to Rome and they brought back from there the Masses and the rule. Again after some time Brigid said to those men, 'I sense that certain things have been changed in the Mass at Rome since you returned from there. Go again'. And they went and they brought back what they found.

91. On a certain rainy day Brigid came to her house. And when the rain had ceased, a ray of the sun came into the house through the wall. And Brigid hung her clothing on that ray, thinking it was a rope. Then someone preached the word of God in that house and Brigid listened carefully to the word of God into the evening and the greater part of the night, her mind intoxicated by the word of God and forgetting present things. But that ray on which Brigid had hung her own wet clothing remained after the setting of the sun until the middle of the night.

Then one of those who were in that house said to Brigid, 'Take your clothing from that ray of light because that ray will not disappear until the morning unless you take your clothing from it'. Then Brigid quickly rose and took her clothing from the beam saying, 'I thought that it was a rope, not a ray'. Others also on that same night came to the plain of the Liffey and said they saw that ray lighting the plain until they reached holy Brigid in the middle of the night. Then everyone gave thanks to God and praised holy Brigid.

92. After these things holy Brigid went out to journey to the region of the Connachtmen with two bishops as companions with her and they lived in Mag Aí.

On a certain day she approached the altar to take the Eucharist from the hand of the bishop and looking inside the chalice she saw in it an ominous shape, that is, she saw the shadow of a goat in the chalice. One of the boys of the bishop was holding the chalice. Then Brigid did not wish to drink from that chalice. And the bishop said to her, 'Why are you not drinking from this chalice?' Brigid showed him what she saw in the chalice.

Then the bishop said to the boy, 'What did you do? Give glory to God'. And the boy confessed that he had committed a theft against a goatherd and had killed one of the goats and eaten part of its meat. The bishop said to him, 'Repent and shed tears with weeping'. And the boy obeyed the commands and repented. Brigid called again, came to the chalice and this time saw nothing of that goat in the chalice. For tears had washed away his guilt.

93. At another time in that same region a certain decrepit and sickly old woman was dying and all the virgins of that place came to her to keep a vigil and pray with her in the home. And holy Brigid came with them.

Then one of the virgins said, 'Let us remove her clothes from her lest she die in them and we have to wash them in the cold and snow'. Holy Brigid forbade this saying, 'She will be with you for only a short time. Show pity to her for a little while'.

When indeed the soul had left the body of the little old woman, her clothes were seen outside and no one saw who had carried them out. For the charity of Brigid's heart desired both that the sick little old woman not be stripped of clothes in the great cold and that the virgins not have to labour in the great cold. So she saved both from the assault of the cold. Then everyone praised God and holy Brigid.

94. When holy Brigid was living in a certain church in the same place, she used to visit a pool of water. One night when there was snow and ice, while everyone was asleep, Brigid came to the pool with a certain nun. And Brigid spent that night in the pool praying and weeping. And what she had done once that night, she wished to do this always every night and turn it into a habit. But the mercy of Christ did not allow it to continue any longer.

For on another night they discovered that pool was dry without water, only with dry sand. But coming back to the pool at dawn, they found it full of water as it had always been. The next night again the pool was dry, but in the days it became full of water. And so God manifested to all the great power of the virgin Brigid.

95. A great discussion arose among the people of Leinster about the absence of holy Brigid and they sent messengers to her in the lands of the Connachtmen to return her to her own people. Then Brigid went with them.

And when they came to the River Shannon, they found there near Áth Luain two groups of people sitting on opposite banks, that is, the Uí Néill and the people of Connacht. Then the nuns of holy Brigid asked everyone to take them across the river in their boats, but had no success. Then a certain very wicked man said to them, 'Give me one of your cloaks and I'll take you across the river in my boat'. And the nuns said, 'No, but we shall go now into the river and the blessing of holy Brigid will protect us'.

At that same time Brigid said to her nuns, 'Make the sign of the cross on that river in the name of Jesus Christ so that it might become calmer and lower for us'. Then holy Brigid, while the two groups of people were standing by, as we said, entered into the river with her nuns, but the deep river didn't reach up to the knees of the virgins which even the strongest men could not cross without a ship. And everyone praised God and holy Brigid.

Now before holy Brigid had entered the river with her nuns, some clerics had gone into a little raft, though they admitted they were inexperienced in sailing, and they said to Brigid, 'This raft is able to carry one of your nuns with us'. Then Brigid told one of the nuns to go ahead of her with them across the river. And the nun said, 'Bless me please, for I fear to be separated from you in the river'. Brigid said to her, 'Go in peace, the Lord will protect you'. Then they set out and in the middle of the river the boat sank with everyone watching. Then the nun who had been put in danger cried out the name of Brigid for help. And Brigid blessed her and prayed for her as she sat on the water. And the water carried her on her seat to the far side with dry clothes. Then everyone praised the wonderous God all-powerful in the holy virgin Brigid.

96. And so when holy Brigid had come to her own country, all the people welcomed her with great honour and rejoicing.

But at a certain time there was little bread for the virgins of Brigid in the place where they were staying. Then a man, good and generous, who lived in the eastern part of the plain of the Liffey came to Brigid and said to her, 'Let your nuns come with me so that they may carry back to you some grain'.

Then they went with him and the nuns returned with their supplies from the man. And when they came to the River Liffey, they found it full beyond the banks with a great flood of water and they were not able to cross the river because of the rising waters. Then the virgins did not know what they should do. They threw themselves onto the earth near the bank of the river and called with one voice on holy Brigid for help. At the same time they were carried from that place in which they were to the other bank of the river with their supplies. And by what way or how they were carried they did not know.

Then the nuns came to holy Brigid and told her the miracle that had happened to them. And she told them to tell this miracle to no one. But it could not be concealed.

97. Holy Brigid had a certain pupil named Darlugdach, who one day when she was not guarding her eyes saw a man and desired him and he also loved her. Then that virgin on a certain night planned to meet the man. That same night though this virgin was in the same bed with holy Brigid.

However after sleeping a little while with holy Brigid, the virgin got up. But when she was getting out of the bed a great confusion of thoughts rushed into her and an indescribable battle raged in her heart, that is, between fear and love. For she feared God and Brigid but also burned vehemently with the fire of love for the man. And so she prayed to the Lord to help her in this great conflict. Then when a good plan came from God, she filled her two shoes with burning coals and fixed her two feet into them. And so it happened that fire extinguished fire and pain conquered pain. And she returned back to her bed.

All these things Brigid sensed, but nonetheless was silent so that the girl might be tested and her character proven. But on the next day the nun confessed her sin. And Brigid said to her, 'How bravely you battled last night! You burned your feet in the present life so that the fire of fornication will not burn you again in the present life nor the fire of hell in the future'.

Then Brigid healed her burnt feet so that not even a trace of the fire remained on them, as if the fire had not touched them.

98. On another day holy Brigid called harvesters to her harvest. And that day was rainy and through that whole province rain poured down abundantly, but her harvest alone remained dry without the hinderance of rain. And although all the harvesters of that region on that day were stopped by rain, her harvesters, without any shadow of darkness, that whole day from the rising of the sun to its setting through the power of God performed their work with fine weather without ceasing.

99. Likewise on another day with three bishops coming and staying with her as guests, although holy Brigid did not have food to feed them, by the manifold miraculous help of God, she milked a single cow against all normal usage three times in one day. And what she was accustomed to milk from three cows, miraculously she milked from her one cow.

A boy knowing about this cow asked holy Brigid to give her to him. But after he took her away she was like all other cows. And whatever cow came to Brigid became like the cow mentioned above.

100. On another day a certain woman came to holy Brigid saying, 'What am I to do about my baby? His father wishes to kill him because he was almost stillborn. He is blind from birth, having a flat face'.

Then Brigid having pity on the woman ordered her to wash the boy's face in water nearby. And immediately the boy, who was called a cretin, was made healthy. And they say that until his death he had no disease of the eyes but had healthy eyes always.

101. And again on another day a certain mischievous boy came to holy Brigid knowing her to be compassionate to the poor. As a joke and at the malicious urging of others, he came dressed as a pauper and asked her for a sheep from her flock. And she gave him a sheep. And he came again seven times, cleverly dressed as a different pauper, asking in the name of the Lord for seven sheep, and got from her what he wanted. But when evening fell and the flock was counted, the number was found to be correct. In addition, when the seven sheep that were the cause of the joke were added to the flock in the night, no surplus was discovered.

102. Also in another miraculous event, lepers came to Brigid asking for beer. And although she didn't have any, seeing water brought in for a bath she blessed it by the power of faith and turned it into the best beer and drew it out abundantly for the thirsty people.

103. On another day holy Brigid, through the most powerful strength of faith, blessed a woman fallen after a vow of integrity and who had a pregnant and swollen womb. With the conception in her womb shrinking without birth and without pain, she restored her to wholeness and repentance. That woman was healed and she gave thanks to God.

104. One day a certain man came asking for salt from Brigid, just as other poor people were accustomed to come pouring out their needs. Holy Brigid however not having salt on hand, poured an abundance of salt made from a stone she had blessed into the hand of the beggar. And thus carrying his salt from her, he went home rejoicing.

105. On another day when holy Brigid was lifting her mind from earthly things to heaven, she gave away a large portion of bacon to a dog. And when that portion was searched for it was found whole and intact not anywhere except where the dog usually was, with a month having passed. For the dog did not dare to eat what had

been given to him by the blessed virgin Brigid. Instead he turned out to be a patient and trustworthy guardian of the bacon contrary to his natural desire and tamed by divine virtue.

106. On another day when a pauper needing food asked her, she went to another man who had cooked meat to ask for some for the pauper. But that very stupid servant who had been cooking the meat placed the portion not yet cooked into her lap, that is, the fold of her white clothing. And when she gave it to the pauper, it had not stained her white clothing but the clothing had maintained its natural colour.

107. And again on another day when a wild boar had fled alone and terrified from the forest, he ran in a wild rush straight into the herd of pigs of the most blessed Brigid. When she saw him among her own swine, she blessed him. Then it remained unafraid and calm in her herd of pigs because even brute animals and beasts were not able to resist her words and wishes. Tamed and happily subject in peaceful servitude to her, they served her as she wished.

108. At another time holy Brigid healed a very strong man named Lugaid who had too great an appetite, who is said to have eaten in one meal an ox and a pig with plenty of bread. By as much as he surpassed men in strength, by that much he also excelled them in eating. And so she gave him an appetite like all other men, with no lessening of his strength.

109. On another night a dear layman with his wife was in the guest house of holy Brigid. And he asked Brigid to make the sign of the cross over the womb of his wife so that he might have a son. And Brigid did so. And on that very night he slept with his wife. From this the remarkable holy Étchén was born.

On that night a certain slave woman stole a silver lunula from the wife of that layman. And on the next day with many people pursuing her, she threw that lunula into a very large river. And a miraculously large fish immediately ate it. In that same hour fishermen caught that fish in their nets and right away brought the fish to holy Brigid as an offering. But when the fish was cut open Brigid gave the lunula to the wife of the layman. Then he with his pregnant wife giving thanks to God and Brigid went on their way.

110. At another time holy Brigid came to another devote virgin. She however having nothing except one calf, prepared dinner for holy Brigid from the calf of her only cow and cooked it on the wood of her loom. Hearing and knowing this, holy Brigid in the morning restored all these things, that is, the calf returned to its mother in the morning and the new loom was discovered as it had been before.

111. At another time holy Brigid gave the vestments for Mass of Bishop Conled to the poor, because she had nothing else to give to them. And right away in that hour of sacrifice, Conled asked for his vestments saying, 'The body of Christ and his blood I do not offer up without my vestments'. Then with Brigid praying, God prepared similar vestments and everyone who saw glorified God.

112. Also at another time holy Brigid sent vestments in a chest across the sea so that they might come over after a long journey to Bishop Senán who was living on another island in the sea. And with the Holy Spirit revealing, he said to his brothers, 'Go as fast as you can to the sea and whatever you discover there bring back here to me'. And they going out found the chest with the vestments as we said. Senán seeing this gave thanks to God and Brigid, for where humans are not able to go without great labour, the chest by itself went guided by God.

113. And also on another day holy Brigid threw a lump of silver into a river so that by that means it might go to another virgin, named Kinna, who a little while before had refused to carry the lump. And thus afterwards, guided by God, she received it.

114. On a certain day another prisoner was led out to be executed by another king. In the hour of his death, with holy Brigid praying, she received silver in her lap from God and gave it to the king for him. And that prisoner was freed from death.

115. Also on another day holy Brigid divided a single tunic between two paupers. And both halves of the tunic in that hour were made a whole tunic by God.

116. On another day the holy woman bored with her fingers into a very hard rock, for she had some great need which we will not mention for the sake of brevity.

117. Holy Brigid also freed the daughter of a certain chieftain, for although she wished to preserve her virginity for God, her father was forcing her to marry. On the night of the wedding banquet preparations, leaving her parents, she fled to holy Brigid. In the morning her father followed her, but when his horses were seen from afar by Brigid she made the sign of the cross on the ground and none of them could move. But as soon as he repented he was released with his men. And thus the daughter was freed from fleshly marriage and joined with Christ, just as she had vowed in her heart.

118. Another proud king rejected a chieftain whom holy Brigid wished to rule in another settlement. And the king immediately fell from his chariot and having struck his head on the earth died.

119. At another time driven by poverty and the arrival of guests, she changed nettles into butter and the bark of trees into the fattest and sweetest bacon.

120. Holy Brigid promised another druid, who had given her his inheritance, that she would come to him in the hour of his death. And so it was done. For when that man lay on his bed waiting for death, he said to his household, 'Take care quickly of everything that is necessary, for I see holy Brigid in white clothing coming to

me with a great crowd'. And thus he was baptized and died believing in God.

121. At a certain time holy Brigid and holy Ita, also named Daritha, were conversing with each other about Christ and did not notice the night. For when Christ the sun of justice was present, he left no darkness.

Then Ita said to Brigid, 'Bless my eyes so that I might see the world just as I wish'. For she was deprived of eyesight. Then Brigid blessed her eyes and immediately they were opened. But holy Ita said, 'Close my eyes again. For by as much as one is absent from the world, by that much more God is present'. And thus again Brigid closed her eyes just as she asked.

122. On another night holy Brigid alone with God helping moved an immovable log of wonderous size, a log that many man had not been able to move earlier. For an angel of God with Brigid moved it to the place that she wanted.

123. One time also a certain woman with her mute daughter came to the church of holy Brigid and called to her another virgin by the name of Darlugdach saying to her, 'Arrange for me so that my foster-daughter might be healed'.

Then she brought the daughter before Brigid saying to her, 'This daughter comes to you. Speak to her'. Then Brigid asked her saying, 'Do you wish to remain a virgin or be joined in marriage?' She did not know that she was mute. Immediately the daughter answered saying, 'Whatever you tell me, I want to do'. And thus afterwards until her death she was more eloquent than anyone.

124. And another day Brigid saw ducks swimming in the water and she called them to come flying through the air to her. They, obedient to her calls and without any fear of the crowd, flew to her. After petting and embracing them for a time, she let them go away.

125. One day a certain peasant, not knowing any better, saw a fox in the hall of a king. Not knowing that it was tame and domesticated and had been trained in various tricks by the king and his companions to provide entertainment, with a crowd watching, he killed it. Then he was bound and led to the king who ordered that man to be killed and his wife and sons and all his household sold into slavery unless he restored to him a fox similar in abilities.

When holy Brigid learned what had happened, moved with compassion and pity, ordering her chariot to be yoked and pouring forth prayers to the Lord for the poor man, she set out on the road leading to the king's settlement. Without delay the Lord pitied him and sent one of his wild foxes to her. It jumped into the chariot, hid itself under Brigid's cloak and sat with her quietly in the chariot.

When Brigid had come to the king, she began to beseech him to release the poor foolish fellow. But the king refused, insisting that he would not release him unless a fox similar in abilities was given to him. Then she brought out her fox before them and doing all things like the other, it performed various tricks before everyone. Then the king was satisfied and dismissed the man to go free.

But when holy Brigid returned to her house after the man was freed, the crafty fox shrewdly running through the crowd returned to the wild places and to its own den. And even with horses and dogs chasing, it escaped unharmed. And everyone who saw admired the power of God through Brigid.

126. When another man came to holy Brigid offering to her fat pigs, he said to her, 'Let some of your companions come with me to my farm so that they bring the pigs to you'. This farm was a long way from the church of holy Brigid, a journey of three or four days.

Then Brigid sent companions with him, but after travelling a journey of one day on a nearby mountain, they saw the pigs, which they thought were far away, coming nearer to them driven and guided along the road by wolves. And when that man understood that his pigs had been driven unharmed by wolves from Mag Fea through dense woods out of reverence for holy Brigid he was amazed and gave glory to God.

And so the next day those who had been sent by Brigid returned home with the pigs telling of the marvellous deed and everyone gave thanks to God.

127. On another day Brigid found honey in the floor of her house which was not there before. But in that hour God granted it to holy Brigid because being in great need of honey she had asked her Lord and thus found it.

128. On another day holy Brigid, through the power of God, moved another river from its place to another place. And the original course of that river until today is visible to people.

129. But when the departure of holy Brigid from this world drew near, her pupil Darlugdach wanted to leave this life with her. Brigid answered saying to her, 'My successor you will be for one year. And on the date of my death you will die so that there will be one feast day for us both'. And thus it happened.

Holy Brigid moved from this light, after her victory, among choirs of patriarchs and prophets and apostles and martyrs and of all holy men and virgins and among the ranks of angels and archangels to the eternal crown of the celestial kingdom, to the heavenly Jerusalem, to the kingdom without end, where eternal rewards are given through our Lord Jesus Christ Your Son.

1. Fuit quidam vir nobilis Laginensis genere nomine Dubthacus.[1] Ille emit ancillam nomine Broicsech[2] et erat formosa forma et moribus bonis et bona seruitute. Concupiuit autem illam dominus suus Dubthacus et dormiuit cum ea quae concepit ab eo in utero. Hoc autem sciens propria uxor Dubthachi contristata est valde et dixit viro suo, 'Eice et vende ancillam istam ne progenies ipsius meam progeniem superat'. Sed vir nolebat vendere ancillam, valde amans eam, in omnibus enim moribus perfecta fuit.

2. Quadam autem die sederunt ambo in curru, vir ille et ancilla, et exierunt secus domum cuiusdam magi. Audiens autem magus sonitum currus, dixit seruis suis, 'Videte quis sedet in curru, currus enim sub rege sonat'. Tunc serui dixerunt, 'Neminem cernimus nisi Dubthacum in curru'. Magus dixit, 'Vocate illum ad me'.

Vocatoque magus dixit, 'Mulier quae postergum tuum sedet in curru, an habet conceptum in utero?' Dubthacus respondens ait, 'Habet'. Magus dixit, 'O mulier, de quo viro concepisti?' Illa[3] respondit, 'De domino meo Dubthacho'. Magus illi[4] dixit, 'Hanc mulierem valde custodi, mirabilis enim erit conceptus illius'. Dubthachus respondit, 'Conpellit me uxor mea ut hanc famulam vendam. Timet enim semen illius'. Magus ait, 'Uxoris tuae semen semini famulae seruiat usque ad finem seculi'. Ad ancillam vero magus dixit, 'Constans esto animo, quia nullus poterit tibi nocere. Gratia enim infantule liberabit te. Claram namque filiam paries quae lucebit in mundo sicut sol in virtice caeli'. Dubthachus dixit, 'Deo gratias ago quia hucusque filiam non habui, sed filios tantum'.

Reuersi sunt Dubthachus et ancilla eius ad domum suam. Dubthachus vero plus dilexit ancillam suam post sermones magi. Tunc uxor irata cum fratribus suis urgebat valde Dubthachum ut venderet ancillam in regionem longinquam.

1   dubdach P, dubthacus Z, dubtachus H, dubtagus M.
2   broicseh L, broicsech P, broisech Z, bochsech H, broihseh M
3   illum L, illa P
4   ille L, illi PZ

3. Illis autem diebus, Deo instigante, duo sancti episcopi ex Precannia[5] venientes intrauerunt domum Dubthachi, quorum unus vocabatur Mel et alter Melchu. Dixitque Mel ad uxorem Dubthachi, 'Quare tristis es? Partus famulae tuae praecellet te et semen tuum. Sed tamen ancillam sicut filios tuos ama, quia progenies illius tuo semini multum proficiet'.

4. Cum ergo uxor perdararet in furore, venit quadam poeta de nepotibus Neil, Deo inspiratus, et emit ancillam Dubthachi. Sed tamen ille non vendidit partum quam habebat illa in utero. Perrexit igitur poeta cum ancilla ad suam regionem. Et in illa nocte in qua intrauit in domum suam venit quidam hospis, sanctus vir, orans Deum per totam noctem. Et videbat ille in nocte sepe globum igneum in locum[6] in quo ancilla dormiebat et hoc mane poete narrauit.

5. Illo tempore venit quidam magus ab aquilonali parte ad domum huius poete et vendidit ancillam istam et dedit mago illo.

6. Quadam autem die magus ille regem suum et reginam inuitauit ad caenam, sed regina illa erat vicina partui. Tunc amici et serui regis interrogabant quendam prophetam quic hora oportebat reginam prolem parere. Magus dixit, 'Si die crastino orto sole nasceretur, neminem in terris haberet equalem'. Sed regina ante horam genuit filium.

Mane autem facto et orto sole, venit ancilla magi ad domum portans vas plenum lacte nuper emulso. Et cum posuisset unum pedem trans limen domus et alterum pedem foris, cecidit super limen sedens et genuit filiam.

Sic enim dixit propheta quod nec in domo nec extra domum ista ancilla pareret. Et de lacte illo calido quod portabat corpus infantis mundatum est.[7]

5   precannia L, pretania Z, britannia PHM.
6   loco PZH
7   mundatus L, mundatum PZHM

7. Post haec autem ille magus cum ancilla perrexit ad regionem Connachtorum[8] et habitauit ibi, quia de Connachtis erat mater illius magi, pater vero de Muminensibus.

Quadam autem die exiit ancilla ista ad mulgendas vaccas procul et reliquid filiam solam dormientem in domo. Tunc domus illa accensa igne apparebat et cucurrerunt omnes ut extinguerent ignem. Et cum appropinquassent domum, ignis non apparauit. Et viderunt puellam letantem in domo pulchra facie et genis rubigundis. Et dixerunt omnes, 'Haec autem puella plena est Spiritu Sancto'.

8. Die autem quadam idem magus et ancilla cum essent ceteri sederunt[9] in loco quodam et subito viderunt pannum contingentem caput puellae flamme ardere incendio et porrigentibus illis manus suas velociter, ignem non viderunt.

9. Die quoque quadam magus dormiens vidit duos[10] clericos vestibus albis indutos effundentes oleum super caput puelle. Ordinem complebant baptismi consueto more. Unus ex illis dixit, 'Hanc virginem vocate Brigitam'.

10. Nocte quadam hic magus erat vigilans, suo more, astra caeli considerans. Et per omnem noctem vidit columnam ignis ardentem consurgentem ex domuncula in qua ancilla cum filia sua dormiebat. Et vocauit ad se aliquem virum et ipse similiter vidit.

11. Quadam autem die audita est vox infantis orans Deum et expandens manus ad caelum. Salutauit eam unus vir et illa respondit, 'Meum erit hoc, meum erit hoc'.

Audiens ille magus dixit, 'Vera prophetia est quae respondit infans quia haec loca illius erunt in aeternum'. Quod postea completum est, nam parrochia magna est hodie sanctae Brigide in illis regionibus.

---

8   connahtorum L, connachtorum P
9   et ceteri cum eis sederunt P
10 tres P

Hoc autem audientes habitatores illius regionis congregauerunt se ad magum dicentes ei, 'Tu mane nobiscum, puella vero quae prophetat, quod regiones nostrae illius erunt recedat a nobis'. Magus respondit, 'Ancillam meam cum filia non relinquam, sed potius terram vestram'. Tunc magus cum suis omnibus perrexit ad patriam suam, quae est in regionibus Muminensium ubi habebat hereditatem patris sui.

Sancta puella cibos fastidiebat magi atque vomebat cottidie. Haec magus considerans scrutabatur causam nausie. Eamque inuenit et dixit, 'Inmundus sum ego. Puella autem ista plena est de Spiritu Sancto. Cibum autem meum non acccipit'.

Deinde elegit vaccam albam et destinauit eam puelle. Et mulgebat eam vaccam aliqua femina Christiana, virgo valde religiosa, et bibebat puella lac illius vacce sanoque ventre non vomuit illud. Et illa femina Christiana nutriebat puellam.

Cum autem creuisset puella sancta, ministrabat in domo et quodcumque manus eius tetigisset vel oculus eius vidisset de cibis, amplius crescebat.

12. Post haec intrauit cogitatio in cor eius ut ad patrem suum rediret. Hoc sciens magus misit nuntios ad illum ut dixissent ei accipere filiam suam liberam. Tunc ille gauisus est valde et venit ad domum magi et duxit filiam suam inde et secuta est eam nutrix sua Christiana.

13. Nutrix eius dolens misit sanctam Brigidam et aliam puellam cum ea ad domum cuiusdam viri ut postularent potum ceruisae aegrotanti. Et nihil inde sumentes ad proprium domum reuersi[11] sunt. Tunc sancta Brigida declinauit ad puteum et impleuit vasculum suum aqua et facta est ceruisa obtima. Et cum gustasset nutrix sua, surrexit sana.

14. Non multo post tempore quidam hospis honorabilis venit ad domum patris sui, cui pater disposuit carnem coquere et dedit filiae

11 reuersae PH

suae quinque particulas ad coquendas eas. Ille autem egressus est foras et hospis vero intus dormiebat.

Tunc venit auidus canis in domum et Brigita dedit ei unam particulam. Et iterum venit canis[12] et dedit ei alteram. Et hoc hospis videbat sed tacebat. Illa vero putabat illum dormire.

Postea venit pater in domum et quinque particulas integras inuenit. Hospis narrauit ei quae vidit et dixerunt ad inuicem, 'Indigni sumus ut hunc cibum comedamus, sed melius est ut detur pauperibus'.

15. Religiosa quaedam vidua in proximo vico habitans postulans a patre eius ut sancta Brigita secum exiret ad sinodum qui collectus fuerat in campo Liffi. Et a patre permittitur illa et egressae sunt viam.

Tunc vir sanctus in sinodo dormiens vidit visionem et surgens ait, 'Vidi Mariam et quendam virum stantem cum ea qui dixit mihi, "Haec sancta Maria quae habitauit inter vos"'.

Et cum haec vir sanctus narrasset in sinodo, statim superuenit vidua cum sancta Brigita. Tunc sanctus dixit, 'Haec est Maria quam vidi quia formam illius manifeste agnosco'.[13] Tunc omnes glorificauerunt eam quasi in typo Mariae.

16. Post haec exiit sancta Brigita ut visitaret matrem suam quam reliquid cum supradicto mago. Sed mater eius in illo tempore separata procul a domo magi erat et xii vaccae cum illa ad colligendum butyrum.

Et postquam venit sancta Brigita ad matrem suam, distribuit butyrum cottidie pauperibus et hospitibus et diuidebat butyrum[14] in xii partes, quasi xii apostolis. Et una pars maior fiebat quasi Christo, illa enim dicebat, 'Omnis hospis Christus est'.

12 alius canis P
13 cognosco HM
14 patrem L, butyrum PZHM

17. Alio die venit magus et uxor illius habentes vas magnum ut impleretur butyro. Videns autem sancta Brigida vas magnum, confusa est verecundie rubore facies eius. Non enim habebat butyrum nisi mensuram unius diei et mensurae semis alterius.

Quibus domum ingressis, laeto animo ministrabat virgo, pedes eorum lauabat cibumque adponens largiter refecit eos. Post haec ingressa in penus suum et orauit Dominum et protulit inde modicum butyri quod habuit.

Videns hoc uxor magi spreuit illud ac subrisit dicens, 'Paruum quod protulisti'. Virgo respondens ait, 'Implete vas butyro quod habetis'. Tunc per potentiam Dei de hoc modico butyro vas magnum impletum est.

Cum videret magus hoc miraculum, ad sanctam Brigitam dixit, 'Hoc vas plenum ignoto butyro tuum fiat et xii vaccae quas mulsisti tuae sint'. Brigita dixit, 'Tuae vaccae tecum sint. Matrem meam mihi liberam relinque'. Magus dixit,[15] 'Ecce offero tibi butyrum et vaccas et matrem tuam liberam'.

Tunc magus credidit Domino et baptizatus est. Sancta vero Brigita omnia oblata sibi a mago dedit pauperibus et reuersa[16] est cum matre ad patrem suum.

18. Post haec cogitabat Dupthachus filiam vendere suam quia multa furta faciebat, omnia enim quae videbat[17] pauperibus occulte dabat.

Quadam autem die adsumpsit eam secum in curru ut irent ad regem. Cumque venissent ad aulam regis, reliquid Dupthachus currum iuxta eam et exiit ad regem. Venitque pauper ad sanctam Brigidam et dedit illi gladium regalem patris sui quem dedit ei rex.

Tunc Dupthacus ad regem dixit, 'Eme filiam meam ut seruiat tibi'. Rex respondit, 'Qua causa vendis eam?' Dupthachus dixit,

15 ait H
16 reuersus L, reuersa PZ
17 habebat P

'Quicquid inuenerint manus eius furatur'. Dixitque rex, 'Illa veniat ad nos'.

Exiit autem Dupthachus ad eam dicens, 'Ubi est gladius meus?' Illa respondit, 'Ego dedi illum Christo'. Iratus autem pater volens interficere virginem. Rex vero ait ad eam, 'Cur dedisti gladium meum et patris tui pauperibus?' Illa respondit, 'Si teipsum et illum Deus meus a me postulasset, si potuissem, vos cum omnibus quae habetis illi darem'.

Tunc rex ait, 'Ista filia, ut video, Dupthache, magna est mihi ad emendum[18] et maior est tibi ad vendendum'.[19] Tunc rex tribuit virgini alium gladium ut daret eum patri suo. Et reuersus est Dupthachus ad domum suam letus cum filia.

19. Non longo tempore post haec venit vir quidam honorabilis ad Dupthachum ut peteret filiam eius in coniugem. Et hoc placuit patri et fratribus. Brigita vero respuebat illum. Cumque graviter conpellerent eam ut viro iungeretur, rogauit sancta Brigita Deum omnipotentem ut aliquam deformitatem super corpus suum daret ut cessarent homines eam quaerere.

Tunc unus oculus illius crepauit et liquefactus est in capite suo. Illa enim magis elegit oculum perdere quam oculum animae et plus amavit pulchritudinem animae quam corporis.

Hoc autem videns pater eius permisit ei velatam esse. Et oculo restituto sanata est accepta velamine ut post dicit.[20]

20. Tunc sancta Brigida, acceptis secum tribus puellis, perrexit ad fines nepotum Neil ad duos sanctos episcopos, Mel et Melchu, qui discipuli sancti Patricii fuerunt et in oppidis Midi[21] illi habitauerunt.

---

18 ad emendum mihi L, magna est mihi ad emendum P
19 maior est ad uendendibus L, maior est tibi ad vendendum P
20 Et oculo restituto sanata est accepta velamine ut post dicit resitituto L, Et oculo restituto sanata est accepta velamine PHM
21 oppidi medi L, opidis midi PH, oppidis medi M

Et habebant quendam discipulum, nomine Mac Caille.[22] Ille[23] dixit ad Mel, 'Ecce sanctae virgines foris sunt quae volunt velamen virginitatis de manu tua accipere'. Tunc introduxit eas ante episcopum. Intuensque illas episcopus Mel, subito apparuit columna ignis de vertice Brigitae usque ad culmen ecclesiae in qua manebat.

Tunc episcopus sanctus Mel posuit velamen super caput sanctae Brigidae. Et lectis orationibus Brigida, capite submisso, pedem altaris ligneum in manu sua tenuit. Et ab hac hora ille pes viridis sine ulla putredine et sine defectu manet in aeternum. Et oculus sanctae Brigitae statim sanatus est dum illa velamen accepit.

Tunc et aliae virgines octo acceperunt velamen simul cum sancta Brigita. Et illae virgines cum suis parentibus dixerunt, 'Noli nos relinquere, sed mane nobiscum et locum habitandi in his regionibus accipe'. Tunc mansit cum illis sancta Brigita.

21. Quadam autem die venerunt ad Brigitam cum puellis suis tres viri religiosi et peregrini et illa refecit eos cibo et cocto lardo. Illi autem viri comedentes cibum abscondentes tres partes lardi, nolentes lardum comedere.

Crastino autem die salutans eos Brigita dixit illis, 'Videte qualem cibum habetis remanentem'. Qui cum aspexissent, viderunt has tres partes lardi quod tres panes essent.

22. Alio autem die duo ex his viris exierunt ad opus necessarium, tertius iunior in domo remansit. Quem cum vidit sancta Brigita dixit ei, 'Cur cum fratribus non existi ad operandum?' Ille respondit, 'Quia unam manum non habeo et operari non possum.' Videns autem Brigita manum eius quia mancus erat, sanauit eum et statim exiit post comites suos ad operandum.

23. Cum autem dies Paschae adpropinquaret, voluit sancta Brigida facere caenam omnibus aecclesiis quae circa se in circuitu

22 macca LM, maccaille P
23 ille LM, qui PH, ille qui Z

oppidorum Midi[24] fuerant. Illa tamen materiam cene non habuit nisi unum modium tantum, penuria enim panis illis temporibus in illa regione erat.

Fecit autem illa ceruisam de isto modio in duobus beluibus, alia enim vasa non habebat. Et divisa est haec cereuisa et portata est ab Brigita octodecem aecclesiis quae in circuitu eius erant. Et eis[25] in Caena Domini et in Pascha et in septimana usque ad clausulum Paschae sufficienter omnibus fuit.

In eadem Pascha ad sanctam Brigitam quidam leprosus venit et ille lepra perfusus[26] a Brigida vaccam postulabat. Illa autem vaccam non habens dixit ei, 'Vis ut Deum rogamus ut a lepra tua sanus fias?' Ille respondit, 'Hoc mihi omnibus donis melius est'.

Tunc sancta virgo benedixit aquam et aspersit corpus leprosi et ille sanatus est. Gratias agens Deo, mansit apud Brigitam usque ad mortem suam.

24. Alia autem die una de puellis sanctae Brigitae dolore aegrotabat grauiterque dolens pusillum calidi lactis postulauit, sed nulla vacca cum eis erat. Hoc audiens sancta Brigita ad alteram puellam dixit, 'Imple fiolam aqua frigida et da aegrotanti bibere'. Et cum hoc fecisset, factum[27] est vasculum plenum lacte calido quasi in illa hora emulsum fuisset. Et cum illa bibisset, sanata est.

25. Due virgines de genere sanctae Brigitae quae paralitice erant et in proximo loco habitabant ad Brigitam miserunt ut veniret ut curaret eas. Tunc ad eas sancta Brigita exiit et benedixit eis salem et aquam. Et illae sumpserunt et sanate sunt. Et sanctam Brigitam ad locum suum consecute sunt.

26. Duo dehinc Precones[28] ceci, cum ministro leproso qui illis duobus ducatum praebebat, venerunt ad sanctam Brigitam et

24 oppidorum medi L, opidorum midi PZH
25 eas L, eis PZ
26 profusus PZ
27 factus L, factum PZM
28 precones L, brittones PH, brettones ZM

steterunt ad ianuas aecclesiae in qua illa erat quaerentes ab ea sanitatem. Et illa dixit eis: 'Expectate paulisper intrateque hospitales[29] et comedite et nos praecabimur pro salute vestra'.

Illi autem indignati dixerunt, 'Infirmos generis tui sanas, nos autem quasi aduenas negligis pro Christo curare'. Tunc illa accepto obprobrio exiit ad eos de aecclesia portans secum benedictam aquam et aspersit eos aqua. Et mundatus est leprosus et inluminati sunt ceci, laudantes Deum et gratias agentes ei.

27. Quadam vero die venit quaedam mulier comitante sibi puella[30] vaccam portans in oblationem Brigitae. Sed vitulus vacce errans in silua densissima remansit. Et non poterant minare vaccam sine vitulo.

Tunc una voce clamauerunt dicentes, 'O Brigata, adiuua nos'. Et statim facta est vacca mitis et sana mente rectoque itinere pergebat usque ad Brigitam. Tunc dixit illis, 'Nolite solliciti esse de vitulo. Adueniat enim post matrem suam sequens vestigia illius'. Quod ita fuit.[31]

28. Alia autem die postquam consummata est septimana Paschae, dixit sancta Brigita puellis suis, 'Si deficit ceruisa quam parauimus solemnitati Paschae? Sollicita enim sum de episcopo nostro Mel et de hospitibus Christi'.

Responderunt puellae dicentes, 'Deus mittet'. Et cum hoc dixissent, venerunt in domum due puellae vas plenum in humeris portantes et dederunt illud vas Brigite ut benediceret solito more. At vero Brigita putans quod ceruisa esset in vase, ait, 'Deo gratias agimus qui dedit ceruisam istam episcopo nostro'.

Et sic facta est illa enim aqua in ceruisam ad instar vini optimi conuersa fuit statim.

29 hospitale ZH
30 comitante L, comitante sibi puella PZ
31 quod ita factum est ut praedixit P, quod ita fuit ut ea praedixit Z

29. Eodem tempore santa Brigita dolore oculorum inmoderato dolore capitis cruciebatur. Hoc audiens episcopus Mel misit ad Brigitam ut venisset ad se ut ambo ad quaerendum medicum perexissent ut curasset eam.

Brigita dixit, 'Corporalem medicum quaerere nolo, sed tamen quod tu vis faciemus'. Factum est autem dum episcopus et Brigita iter agerent ad quaerendum medicum, cecidit santa Brigida de curru suo in vado cuiusdam fluminis et vulneratum est caput eius lapide et sanguis vehementer fluebat. Et de illo sanguine mixto cum aqua sanate sunt duae mulieres mute et solute sunt linguae eorum.

Accidit autem post haec ut ille medicus quem quaerebant occurret eis in via. Qui cum manu tetigisset caput virginis dixit, 'O virgo, medicus tetiget caput tuum qui multo melior me est. Nullum enim locum conuentiorem ex quo effunderet et sanguine habuit. Illum medicum semper quaere qui potest morbum ex te repellere'.

Tunc episcopus dixit ad eam, 'Nequaquam iterum ego hortabor te medicum quaerere corporalem'.

30. Post haec autem episcopi Mel et Melchu cum sancta Brigita perrexerunt in campum Tethbe[32] quia illic episcopi monasterium grande habuerunt.

Cumque sancta cum sanctis ibidem moraretur, quadam die rex Tethbe haut procul ab eis fuit in conuiuio. Et rusticus quidam cum tolleret de mensa regis quoddam pretiosum facturae mirabilis et materiae pretiosae et hoc vas apud veteres vocabatur septiformis calix illud cecidit de manu rustici et fractum est.

Tunc iratus rex iussit eum alligari ut occideretur. Hoc audiens episcopus Mel perrexit ut rogaret pro misero, sed rex non dimisit eum. Tunc Mel, portans secum fragmenta vasis confracti, venit ad sanctam Brigitam. Et illa rogauit Deum et restauratum est vas et regi datum est et miser liberatus est. Et fama sanctae Brigidae illam regionem impleuit.

32 tehtbe L, tethbe P, thetbe Z, tehtfe H

31. Erat autem in illa regione quaedam sancta virgo nobilis, Brigita nomine, quae misit ad sanctam Brigitam ut ad domum suam veniret. Tunc Brigida exiit ad domum illius. Et illa suscepit sanctam Brigitam cum gaudio magno et lauit pedes eius. Et de illo lauacro pedum eius sanata est quaedam virgo quae in illo domo iacebat aegrotans et statim surrexit et ministrabat cum ceteris.

Et cum appositus esset cibus, coepit sancta Brigita diligenter mensam intueri. Tunc sancta virgo Brigida ad sanctam Brigitam dixit, 'Quid diligentius intendis?' Respondit Brigita, 'Demonem sedentem in mensa nostra aspicio'. Dixitque Brigida, 'Si possibile est, volo videre illum'. Respondit Brigita, 'Non illud inpossibile, sed prius signentur oculi tui ut possis sustinere faciem eius aspicere'.

Signatisque oculis, vidit inimicum tetra et nigra figura capite ingenti et per omnes fores eius flamma et fumus exalabat. Tunc sancta Brigita dixit ad illum, 'Loquere nobis daemon'. At ille respondit dicens, 'O sancta virgo Brigita, non possim tibi loqui nec tua iussa contemnere quia tu praecepta Dei non contemnis et pauperibus ipsius et minimis efabilis[33] es'.

Dixitque Brigita, 'Qua causa huc venisti?' Demon respondit, 'Apud virginem hic habito et causa pigritudinis eius locum in ea habeo. Venienteque illa virgine huc ut benediceretur, hic remansi'.

Tunc vocata est ad eas illa virgo et signauit oculos eius et vidit horridum monstrum et illa timuit et tremuit. Dixitque ad eam sancta Brigita, 'Vide quem nutrire solebas multis annis'. Et ex illa die liberata est illa virgo a demone.

32. Quadam die in campo Tethbae quaedam mulier munusculum pomorum sanctae Brigidae attulit. Et in eadem hora priusquam mulier de domo exiret, venerunt leprosi postulantes.

Tunc Brigita dixit, 'Diuidite illis haec poma'. Hoc audiens, illa mulier rapuit a se sua poma dicens, 'Tibi et tuis virginibus haec poma attuli, non leprosis'. Hoc displicuit sanctae Brigite et dixit,

33 affabilis PH

'Male agis prohibens elemosinam dare. Ideo ligna tua fructum non habebunt in aeternum'.

Et sic fuit. Tunc illa foras egressa conspexit ortum suum et nullum pomum in eo inuenit quem, in eadem hora plenum pomis reliquerat. Et sterilis in eternum permansit.

33. Alio post tempore sancta Brigida iter agebat per campum Tethbe sedens in curru. Tunc illa vidit quendam maritum cum sua uxore et tota familia et cum multis pecoribus laborantes et portantes onera grauia in ardore solis lassi fuerunt.

Tunc Brigita miserta erat illis[34] deditque eis equos currus sui ad onera portanda. Illa autem remansit iuxta viam sedens cum puellis suis. Dixitque illis Brigita, 'Fodite sub cespite propinquo ut erumpat aqua foras. Venient enim aliqui qui[35] habent escas et sine potu sitiunt'. Tunc foderunt et erupit fluuius.

Post paulolum[36] per eandem viam venit alius dux cum multa turba peditum et equitum. Et ille audiens quod sancta Brigita de equis, obtulit duos equos ei indomitos. Sed statim domiti facti sunt quasi semper essent sub curru.

Post haec venerunt per eandem viam discipuli et familia sancti Patricii episcopi dixeruntque ad sanctam Brigitam, 'Nos in via laboramus. Cibum habemus sed potus deest'. Tunc comites Brigite dixerunt, 'Nos vobis praeparauimus potum fluminis aque. Praedixit enim sancta Brigita vos futuros esse'.

Tunc omnes comederunt et biberunt in commune gratias agentes Deo et Brigitam glorificantes.

34. Duo viri leprosi secuti sunt sanctam euntem cum turba multa quos illa, ut solita erat, benigne accepit. Rixabantur vero miseri et se inuicem percutiebant. Manus illius qui prius percussit proximum incuruata non potuit iterum erigi. Alterius quoque dextera ad repercutiendum sursum erecta recuruari in sinum non potuit.

34 miserta est illorum P, miserata illorum est Z
35 quia L, qui PZH
36 paululum P

Riguerunt igitur manus miserorum manentes inmobiles donec sancta Brigita aduenit. Tunc illi leprosi penitentiam egerunt sanauitque Brigita manus eorum.

35. Alio quoque die currus sanctae Brigitae conductus est ut in eo vir infirmus veheretur qui in extremo confinio vite anhelabat. Cumque infirmus in curru sanctae Brigitae portaretur, venerunt ad vespere ad locum ubi sancta Brigita fuit. Et in illa nocte levius habuit infirmus.

Et in crastino die benedicens eum sanus ambulauit, illa succurrente.[37] Veneruntque leprosi postulantes illum currum et datus est eis cum equis suis.

36. Sancta Brigida rogata ad aliam eclesiam in regione Tethbe exiit ut ibi caelebraret diem Paschae. At vero domina aeclesiae illius puellis suis in die caenae Domini dixit, 'Quae ex vobis hodie lauacrum faciet senibus et infirmis nostris?' Et omnes iuuencule nolentes excusauerunt.

Tunc Brigita dixit, 'Volo ut ego miseras et infirmas abluam'. Erant autem in una domo quatuor egrotae: una paralitica quae iacebat inmobilis, alia vero inergumina demone plena, tertia caeca, quarta leprosa. Tunc Brigita coepit prius lauare paraliticam. Et illa ait, 'O sancta Brigida, roga Christum ut sanet me'. Et orauit Brigita et statim illa sanata est, leprosa mundata est, demens puella sanata est.

37. Ab alia quoque aecclesia regione in eadem rogata est sancta Brigita ut ibi maneret aliquibus diebus. Sed casu accidit ut omnis familia exiret remansitque Brigita cum solo puero muto et paralitico. Nesciebat quod mutus ille et paraliticus esset.

Et in eadem hora venerunt laici quaerentes cibum. Dixitque Brigita ad puerum iacentem, 'Nosti ubi est clauis coccine?' Ille dixit, 'Scio'. Brigita dixit, 'Surge et da mihi eam'. Surrexit et dedit ei clauem et ille ministrabat cum ea cibum hospitibus istis.

37 succurente L, illa succurente P, succurente sancta brigida Z, succurentes HM

Aduenit familia et mirabantur puerum loquentem et ambulantem, et narrauit quomodo sanatus est. Tunc omnes gratias Deo egerunt.

38. Tunc sancti episcopi Mel et Melchu dixerunt ad sanctam Brigitam, 'Vis ut nobiscum pergas in campum Breg ad sanctum episcopum Patricium salutandum?' Brigita respondens ait, 'Ego volo ipsum alloqui ut benedicat me'.

Tunc perrexerunt in viam episcopi et sancta Brigida. Sed rogauit eos quidam clericus habens multam familiam et vaccas et carros et onera multa ut cum illis exiret in campum Breg. Sed nolebant episcopi ne tardaret et iter eorum multitudine pecorum et onerum. Dixitque ad eos Brigita, 'Pergite ante nos. Nam ego remanebo et conpatiar istis'. Tunc remansit illa.

Dixitque famulis, 'Cur non ponitis onera in carras?' Illi aiunt, 'Quia frater noster paraliticus et soror ceca in carris iacent aegroti'. Nocte itaque veniente comederunt et biberunt.[38] Sola vero Brigita ieiunauit et vigilauit. Mane autem illa effudit rorem matutinum super pedes paralitici et statim ille sanus surrexit et ceca femina inluminata est. Tunc inponunt onera in carras et iter inceptum agebant, gratias Deo agentes.

Et cum ambularent in via, viderunt quendam plebeum qui nimio labore solus mulgebat vaccas. Dixitque Brigita, 'Interrogate eum cur solus laborat sine adiutore?' Ille dixit, 'Quia tota familia mea in dolore est. In una enim domo XII aegroti iacent'. Tunc dixit Brigita puellis ut cum eo mulgerent vaccas. Tunc plebeus rogauit ut prandium pro labore acciperent. At illi acceperunt et comederunt iuxta ripam cuiusdam fluminis, praeter solam Brigitam ieiunantem. Tunc sancta Brigita benedixit aquam et aspersit domum plebei et sanauit omnes aegrotos qui in eo fuerunt.

38 dormierunt PZH

39. Inde via recta venerunt ad locum qui vocatur Tailtiu.[39] Ibi sanctus episcopus[40] cum multorum episcoporum conuentu sedebat. Et in illo concilio magna[41] questio fiebat. Quaedam autem virgo quae in peccatum cecidit dicebat infantem quem genuit quod esse cuiusdam episcopi de discipulis sacti Patricii nomine Broon. Ille autem negabat.

Tunc omnes qui erant in concilio, audientes mirabilia opera sanctae Brigite, dixerunt quid haec quaestio per illam sanari potest. Adducta est itaque mulier cum suo infante[42] in sinu ad Brigitam extra concilium.

Dixit ad illam Brigita, 'De quo concepisti hunc infantem?' Illa respondit, 'De episcopo Broon'. Brigita dixit, 'Non sic estimo'. Tunc Brigita ad sanctum Patricium humilians se dixit, 'Pater, tuum est hanc quaestionem soluere'. Patricius respondens ait, 'Mea filia carissima sancta Brigita, reuelare digneris'.

Sancta itaque Brigita significavit os illius feminae signo crucis Christi et statim intumuit totum caput eius cum lingua, sed nec illa paenituit. Tunc Brigida linguam infantis benedixit dicens ei, 'Quis est pater tuus?' Ille respondit ambulans, 'Non est episcopus Broon pater meus, sed quidam homo qui sedet in extrema parte concilii ultimus ac turpis vilisque'.

Tunc omnes gratias egerunt Deo et Brigita magnificata est. Et mulier penitentiam egit.

40. Die illa vesperescente abierunt omnes huc illucque in villus suus. Brigita vero cum suis puellis ad aquam perrexit.

Tunc quidam plebeus inuitauit eam dicens, 'Habeo domum nouam. Volo ut tu cum tuis prima introeas in eam ad consecrandam'. Exiit sancta Brigida cum eo et ministrabat ei cum

39 tultui L, tailtiu P
40 patricius P
41 magnum L, maxima P, magna Z
42 fante L, infante PZH

maximo gaudio, ipse enim vidit virtutem quam in illa die Brigita in concilio fecit et apposuit cibum.

Tunc sancta Brigita puellis suis dixit, 'Ostendit mihi Dominus quod iste vir gentilis est'. Responditque unus de comitibus suis dicens, 'Verum est quod dicis, nam ille prae cunctis sancto Patricio et suis discipulis valde resistit et baptizari rennuit'.

Tunc Brigita dixit ad illum, 'Non possumus cibos tuos comere nisi prius baptizatus fueris'. Tunc, a Deo conpunctus, credidit cum omni domo sua et baptizatus est ab episcopo Broon, discipulo Patricii.

Sequenti autem die dixit Patricius ad Brigitam, 'Ex hac die nec licet tibi ambulare sine sacerdote. Auriga tuus semper sacerdos fiat'. Ordinauitque sacerdotem nomine Nathfroich[43] et ipse in tota vita sua auriga sancta Brigita fuit.

41. In illis diebus venit ad sanctam Brigitam quidam laicus portans matrem suam paraliticam in humeris suis. Et cum ille peruenisset ad locum ubi erat Brigita in curru suo, deposuit matrem in terram super[44] umbram sanctae Brigidae. Et cum illa tetigisset umbram, surrexit dicens, 'Gratias ago Deo quia quando tetigi umbram tuam, O sancta Dei, sanata sum statim nihil dolens'.

Cuius temporis interuallo venerunt ad sanctam Brigidam quidam viri deducentes hominem demoniacum vinculis alligatum. Qui cum cognouisset quod ad Brigidam duceretur, cecidit in terram dicens, 'Non me portabitis ad Brigitam'. Dixeruntque ei, 'Numquid nosti locum in quo Brigita sedet?' Ille respondit, 'Scio et statim noui et ad illum non ibo'. Dixitque illis proprium nomen loci in quo Brigita fuit et non potuerunt commouere illum de terra.

Tunc consilio facto perrexerunt alii ex ipsis ad sanctam Brigitam et rogauerunt eam ut veniret ad illum. Venitque Brigita cum eis. Et cum vidisset demon Brigitam ad se de longe venientem, ab homine

43 natfroich L, nathfroich P, natfiroih Z, natfro H
44 subtus P, super Z, sub H

fugit. Demones enim quando sanctam Brigidam ad loca eorum venire aliunde videbant, timebant et fugiebant. Et sanus factus est ille homo et gratias Deo egit.

42. Eodem tempore hospitabatur sancta Brigida in aeclesia sanctae Lasre. Quadam autem die ad vesperum venit sanctus Patricius cum turba magna ut hospitaretur in illa ecclesia.

Tunc familia loci illius commota est dixeruntque ad Brigitam, 'Quid faciemus quia non habemus cibos ad tantam turbam?' Dixitque illis sancta Brigida, 'Quantum habetis?' Qui dixerunt illi, 'Non habemus nisi duodecim panes tantum et modicum lactis et unam ouem quam coximus in escam tibi et tuis'. Dixitque Brigita, 'Sufficienter haec nobis plurimis erunt, recitabuntur enim nobis sacre scripture per quas carnales escas obliuiscemur'.

Tunc ergo ex illo modico cibo comederunt simul duo populi, id est Patricii et Brigite, et saturati sunt. Et dimiserunt maiores reliquias quam ante fuerunt materiae quae sancta Lasrea obtulit. Et postea obtulit se Lasrea sancta et suum locum sanctae Brigite in aeternum.

43. Ibidem quoque cum sancta Brigita hospitaretur, venit quidam maritus rogans ut sancta Brigita benediceret ei aquam qua conspergeretur uxor sua. Ipsa enim uxor odiuit illum maritum. Tunc Brigita benedixit aquam et aspersa est domus illius et cibus et potus et lectulum de aqua, uxore absente. Et ex illa die uxor dilexit maritum nimio amore quamdiu vixit.

44. In diebus illis venit ad sanctam Brigitam quaedam virgo Dei de nepotibus Guais[45] quaerens elemosinam ab omni domo. Dixitque ad eam Brigita, 'Sagum meum portabis vel vaccam ab aliquo mihi commodatam'. Illa dixit, 'Non prodest mihi ista recipere. Venient enim latrones in via et auferent ea ex me'. Dixitque Brigita, 'Zonam meam portabis. Dixisti enim mihi multos morbos esse in regione

45 gais LZHM, guais P

vestra et per zonam meam intinctam in aqua in nomine Christi Iesu sanabis eos, et dabunt tibi victum et vestimentum'.

Tulit ergo zonam et primum exiit ad alium puerum egrum quem diligebant parentes et sanauit eum. Et data sunt ei vestimenta bona. Sic faciebat per omnes annos vitae suae. Sanauit enim omnes languores et accipiebat multa lucra. Et de illis lucris emit agros et diues effecta fuit et pauperibus tribuebat.

45. Ante diem cuiusdam solemnitatis venit ad sanctam Brigitam in Cella Roboris una discipularum eius quam Brigita nutriuit, portans illi elemosinam. Cumque adsignasset donum, dixit, 'Reuertar ad domum meam ut veniant parentes orare tecum per noctem istam. Ego autem remanebo ad custodiendam domum et pecora'. Brigita dixit, 'Non sic sed tu mane hic et parentes veniant huc. Substantiam autem vestram et domum Dominus seruabit'. Veneruntque parentes sicut illa dixit et simul omnes caelebrauerunt festum apud sanctam Brigitam.

Media vero nocte fures venerunt ad domum eorum scientes habitatores exisse ad sanctam et furati sunt boues. Cumque venissent ad amnem Liffi, inuenerunt flumen repletum abundatiae aquae et non potuerunt boues minare trans flumen.

Cumque laborarent maxima parte noctis, consilio facto alligauerunt omnia vestimenta sua super capita boum similiter et arma sua. Et dimidio flumine retro uersi sunt portantes[46] spolia et arma inimicorum suorum super capita sua currentesque per campum Liffi et viri nudi post eos. Non ad propriam domum boves reuersi sunt, sed recto cursu ad ciuitatem Brigite. Primo diluculo venerunt et cognouerunt multi illos boues et fures.

Tunc fures dederunt laudem Deo et fuerunt in paenitentia apud sanctam Brigidam in sua ciuitate. Plebeus vero exultans cum bubus suis ad domum suam exiit et Deo gratias egit.

46 portans L, portantes PZ

46. Alia quoque puella ante diem cuiusdam festi pari cum elemosina ad sanctam Brigitam venit. Accepto munere ipsius dixit, 'Vadam ad domum meam quia non reliqui in ea nisi nutritorem meum qui est senex valde et paraliticus et non est qui mulgeat vaccas vel domum custodiat'. Sancta Brigita dixit, 'Mane hic hac nocte. Deus custodiat domum tuam et vaccae tuae inmulse fiant'.

Tunc illa mansit et crastina die, sumpta Eucharistia, rediit vaccasque et vitulos separatim in agris comedentes sana mente et sine tedio inuenit. Senemque vidit sine somno qui hucusque non vidit noctem nec dormiuit nec sensit interuallum temporis ac si in illa hora ab eo puella exisset. Et tunc puella gratias Deo egit et glorificauit Brigitam.

47. In illo tempore sancta Brigita magnam caenam fecit in honorem solemnitatis Domini, sed hanc caenam diuisit pauperibus. De hoc vero familia ipsius contristata est, plebsque, ut consueuerat, venit ad diem festum. Tunc Brigita orauit Dominum.

Ecce in eadem regione quidam plebeus homo diues valde caenam regi suo vehebat in plaustro in diem festum. Illeque errauit in suis viis et nebula texit eum et viam ante cognitam non agnouit donec recto cursu ad ianuam eclesiae sanctae Brigitae peruenit.

Hoc sciens sancta Brigita exiit in obuiam illius et interrogauit viam eius. Ille autem ammonitus a Deo obtulit haec omnia sanctae Brigitae dicens, 'Ob hanc causam fecit me Dominus errare in propria mea patria. Aliam vero caenam regi faciam'.

Hoc autem cum rex audisset illum plebeum cum suis omnibus ut seruiret Brigitae in aeternum dedit. Plaustrum quoque alterum plenum ciborum ad sublementum sancte solennitati idem rex ad sanctam Brigitam misit. Quibus ingens conuentus totius plebis saturatus est valde.

48. Regina quaedam ad sanctam Brigitam cum donis bonis venit in quibus erat argentea catena fabrefacta quae habebat in summitate formam hominis. Hanc catenam puellae rapuerunt et absconderunt in thesauris suis. Brigita vero omnia pauperibus diuisit.

Quadam autem die venit quidam pauper ad Brigitam et illa, nihil habens, exiit ad thesaurum puellarum et inuenit ibi catenam praedictam et eam dedit pauperi. Hoc puelle agnoscentes venerunt ad Brigitam dicentes, 'Perdidimus per te cuncta quae Deus misit nobis omnia enim das pauperibus et nos inopes relinquis'.

Tunc sancta Brigita dixit illis, 'Quaerite statim catenam ubi ego iugiter oro in aecclesia. Forsitan illam ibi inuenietis'. Cumque quaererent eam inuenerunt illic catenam eiusdem forme ostenderuntque eam Brigite. Tunc Brigita dixit eis, 'Nonne dixi vobis "Quaerite eam"?' Et puelle hanc catenam semper secum seruauerunt in testimonium virtutis et non vendiderunt[47] eam umquam.

49. Cellanus[48] sanctus episcopus et propheta Dei, qui habebat in dextera parte Liffi campi, venit in curru ad sanctam Brigitam et moratus est apud eam aliquantis diebus.

Quadam die ille volens redire ad locum suum, dixit ad Brigitam, 'Benedic diligenter currum meum'. Et illa benedixit. Auriga vero illius episcopi iungens currum oblitus est rossetos ponere contra rotas. Tunc currus et ipse velos pertransiuit campum.

Cumque post magnum spatium diei, episcopus conspexisset currum, vidit illum rossetos non habere. Tunc ille desiliuit de curru et corruens in terram gratias egit Deo et benedixit sanctam Brigitam, commemorans benedictionem eius.

50. Quadam autem die venit sancta Brigita per campum Liffi et alia sancta virgo simul secum sedens in uno curru. Auriga autem praedicabat illis verbum Dei. Dixitque illi Brigita, 'Noli verso vultu a nobis praedicare verbum Dei. Abenas tuas post tergum tuum pone. Equi enim nostri recto itinere ibunt ad domum nostram'.

Et ita factum est. Exierunt equi recta via per campum. Cumque auriga diligenter praedicaret virginibus et illae intentis auribus et

---

47 uiderunt L, uendiderunt P
48 cellanus LP, collanus Z, coailanus H, gallanus M

animo curioso audirent, unus equus abstulit caput suum et collum ab iugo et ambulabat liber post currum illis nescientibus.

Tunc rex quidam sedebat secus viam in sublimi loco dixitque ille circa sedentibus et mirantibus, 'Brigita orans sedet isto curru equorum oblita. Dominum solum animo intendit'. Tunc equus audiens clamorem turbae admirantis venit ad currum et posuit collum sub iugo solus. Tunc clamor regis et plebis adtollit,[49] et miranda virtus per totam regionem diuulgata est, et glorificauerunt Deum et Brigitam.

51. Leprosus quidam de nepotibus Neil venit ad Brigitam quaerens ab ea vaccam. Dixitque illa armentario, 'Da illi vaccam'. Dixitque armentarius, 'Qualem vaccam illi dabo?' Brigita dixit, 'Optimam vaccam et optimum vitulum da ei'.

Tunc elegerunt optimum vitulorum et dimittentes eum occurrit ei cum gemitu optima vaccarum et tantum se inuicem ambo dilexerunt ut pene nullus potuit separare eos. Vacca etiam illa cuius vitulus portatus est alterius vacce vitulum dilexit vicissim ut suum.

Dixit leprosus ille ad Brigitam, 'Non possum solus vaccam minare ad prouinciam meam'. Dixitque Brigita ad aurigam suum, 'Vade cum leproso'. Erat autem in illa hora auriga coquens carnes in caccabo. Dixit auriga, 'Quis coquet carnes istas?' Brigita dixit, 'Tu ipse ad eas velociter veni'.

Et ita completum est sicut illa[50] dixit. Exiit autem auriga cum leproso iter duorum dierum in uno puncto temporis in eodem puncto confestim reuersus est et inuenit carnes istas in caccabo necdum coctas esse. Et omnes mirati sunt quod auriga potuit iter duorum dierum in unius horae puncto transcurrere. Sed Deus donauit voluntati sanctae Brigide.

52. Erat inopia panis in campo Liffi in alio tempore. Brigita autem rogata a sua familia quaere grana et ad campum Gesilli pergere ad

49 adtollitur Z
50 illud L, illa P

sanctum Iborum episcopum ut peteret ab eo fruges. Brigita obediuit voluntati roganti vero exiuit in viam.

Sanctus vero Iborus gauisus est gaudio magno in aduentu sanctae Brigite, sed tamen ille non habebat cibos in aduentu hospitum nisi panem siccum et carnem suillam. Tunc panem et lardum Iborus episcopus et sancta Brigita in tempore quadragesimae[51] ante Pascha manducauerunt.

Due virgines de comitibus Brigite partes suas non manducauerunt, et ille partes verse sunt in duos serpentes. Hoc quando nuntiatum est sancte Brigite, illas virgines grauiter coram Iboro increpauit et iussit eas foras manere et ieiunare cum lacrimis. Dixitque Brigita, 'Ieiunemus et nos cum illis et oremus Deum'. Et ita fecerunt. Et versi sunt isti duo serpentes in duas oblationes mundissimi et candidissimi panis. Et data est una oblatio Iboro episcopo et altera oblata sancte Brigite. Et fuerunt oblationes Eucharistie in Pascha et in Natalicia Domini.

Dixitque Iborus episcopus sanctae Brigidae, 'Qua causa venisti huc in tempore quadragesimae?' Respondit Brigita, 'Ut quaeram a te annui panis'. Tunc Iborus subridens dixit, 'O Brigida, si tu videres et scires quantum de frugibus habemus. Modicum donum granorum tecum non portabis'. Dixit Brigita, 'Non puto sic. Sed xxiiii plaustra in horreo vestro consistunt'.

Et ita nutu Dei creuit minimum quod Iborus habuit et inuenta sunt ibi xxiiii plaustra sicut Brigita dixit. Et diuiserunt inter se xii plaustra Iboro et Brigita cum xii plaustris reuersa est ad domum suam.

53. Rex quidam venit ad Brigitam ad solemnitatem caelebrandam Pentecosten. Et cum ibi caelebrasset noctem illam, surrexit valde diluculo ut iret ad domum suam. Currebant velociter in curribus et in equitibus. Sancta vero Brigita, post expleta dies solemnia, venit ad mensam et largus cibus apponitur cunctis.

---

51 xlme L, quadragesimae PH

Lommanus,[52] vero leprosus superbissimus, diaboli magisterio sancte Brigide cibum, ut solebat, respuit nisi Brigita sibi daret astam supradicti regis, qui primo mane reuersus est ad domum suam. Omnes leprosi dixerunt, 'Vidisti astam heri. Cur non postulasti statim eam tibi dari?' Ille dixit, 'Quia hodie coepi concupiscere'.

Tunc sancta Brigita et omnes rogauerunt illum ut comederet et non impetrauerunt. Brigita quoque abnuit cibum sumere donec leprosus proteruus comederet. Tunc misit Brigita equites post regem ut rogarent ab eo astam suam. Illi currebant et transeuntes unum montem inuenerunt illum regem in vado cuiusdam fluminis et indicauerunt suam quaestionem. Tunc laetatus[53] est rex et dedit eis astam suam dicens, 'Si sancta Brigita omnia arma mea petisset, statim impetrasset'.

Tunc equites illi missi a Brigita interrogauerunt, 'Ubi moratus es rex ab initio diei usque ad hanc horam nonam'. Dixitque illi cum suis comitibus, 'Non morati sumus sed semper velociter iter currimus. Scimus enim quod sancta Brigita nutu Dei retinuit nos ut cito solueretur inminens questio leprosi'.

Tunc omnes laudauerunt Dominum et Brigitam. Et rex velociter exiit viam suam, non ut ante. Et missi confestim reuersi sunt ad Brigitam cum asta regis, et illa gratias Deo egit.

54. Cum autem esset Brigita in aecclesia quadam et cum sedisset iuxta ianuam loci illius, vidit ad ripam fluminis hominem ambulantem in valle incuruum sub onere. Misertaque illum dixit puellis suis, 'Eamus ad hominem et cum eo onus portemus euntes'.

Dixit illi Brigita, 'Da nobis onus quod te grauat et valde te incuruat'. Respondens ille dixit, 'Non onus incuruat me sed dolor antiquus a iuuentute mea'. Ille homo interrogauit nomen virginis, et dictum est ei quod sancta Brigita esset. Ille dixit, 'Deo gratias ago quia olim quaesitam inueni. Volo ut nocte et die ieiunas et roges

52 lammanus L, lommanus P, iam uero manens Z, iam vero HM
53 letus L, laetatus PZH

Deum ut erigatur corpus meum'. Dixitque illi Brigita, 'Veni ad hospicium et requiesce in eo in hac nocte, et faciam quod vis'.

Tunc sancta Brigita in illa nocte ieiunauit et orauit Dominum pro eo. Mane autem facto exiit ad hospitium et dixit incuruato homini, 'Vade ad aquam fluminis et laua te in nomine Saluatoris et roga Deum erigesque ceruicem et ne descendas donec dicam tibi'. Et sicut illa dixit ita fecit ille et sanatus est et gratias egit Deo qui se erexit curuatum annis xvi.[54]

55. Post haec autem exiit sancta Brigita cum sancto Patricio episcopo ad aquilonalem partem Hiberniae.

Quadam die sanctus Patricius verbum Domini praedicabat suis hominibus, sed in illa hora sancta Brigita dormiuit. Et postquam vigilauit, dixit illi Patricius, 'O Brigita, cur non euigilasti in verbo Christi?' Ut haec ut audiuit, veniam petens genua flexit dicens, 'Parce mihi, pater. Parce, domine sancte. Nam in hac hora somnium vidi'. Et dixit Patricius, 'Narra nobis illud'. Dixit Brigita, 'Ego tua ancilla vidi iiii aratra arantia hanc insulam et seminatores seminauerunt semen. Et statim illud creuit et maturescere cepit et riui lactis noui impleuerunt sulcos. Et seminatores illi induti erant vestibus albis. Post haec vidi alia aratra et aratores nigros, qui bonam illam messem euerterunt et sciderunt vomere et zizania seminauerunt et flumina aquarum repleuerunt sulcos'.

Dixitque Patricius, 'O virgo, veram et mirificam visionem vidisti. Nos sumus boni aratores qui iiii euangeliorum aratris corda humana scindimus et seminamus verbum Dei et lac rudis doctrinae. In fine vero saeculi venient mali doctores malis hominibus consentientes qui nostram doctrinam per omnia subuertent et pene omnes homines seducent'.

56. Alia quoque die quidam leprosus venit ad sanctam Brigitam rogans ut cum ea sua vestimenta lauarentur aqua. Dixitque ei Brigita, 'Faciam quod petis'. Aitque leprosus, 'Non habeo alia

vestimenta nisi mea propria lauentur'. Dixitque Brigita ad unam puellarum suarum, 'Da vestem tuam leproso donec vestes eius mundentur'.

Sed illa puella inobediens fetore nimio et lepra percussa est spatio unius hore. Alia vero puella dedit sagum suum leproso. Tunc leprosus, postquam exuit se a vestimentis suis, mundatus est a lepra sua.

57. In illo tempore post hec cepit sancta Brigida cum puellis suis locum aecclesiae in campo Hinis iuxta habitationem Patritii. Ac dein diebus quadragesimae penuria panis imminebat.

Quadam autem nocte octo viri fures venerunt ut furatentur iiii equos quos Brigita cum suis habebat. Tunc virginum una quae erat sine somno dixit ad Brigitam, 'Equi nostri furto tolluntur'. Dixit Brigita, 'Sine, ego sentio. Plures et fortiores sunt quam nos qui auferant eos'.

Tunc fures ablatis iiii equis exierunt ad domum cuiusdam viri habitantis in proximo loco in plebe et intrauerunt in horreum et inuenerunt in eo L modios seminis ventilatos. Et furati sunt totum hunc numerum modiorum portantes in iiii equis et in propriis humeris suis et venerunt ad habitaculum virginum, putantes enim se[55] quod ad propriam domum venissent. Et intrauerunt in paruum tugurium alligantes equos in angulo secreto et somno graui dormierunt post vigilias.

Facto autem mane, ecce viri venerunt a quibus grana rapta sunt ad habitaculum virginum dixeruntque ad Brigitam, 'Fures furati sunt grana nostra et duximus vestigia furorum et equorum usque ad ianuam vestri. Oramus ne celetis eos'. Tunc exiit sancta Brigita ad fures et suscitauit eos dicens, 'Cur furtum adtulistis ad nos?' Illi autem dixerunt, 'Quia putabamus quod ad nostram domum venimus'.

Tunc sancta Brigita misit ad Patricium episcopum in proximo manentem. Venitque ad eos statim Patricius et fures liberati sunt et

55 omit P

penitentiam egerunt. Et alii obtulerunt sua grana Brigite cum suis virginibus, sciebant enim quod a Deo donata sunt eis virginibus.

58. Sanctus Patricius quadam die praedicabat verbum Dei turbis et sanctae Brigidae. Tunc omnes viderunt nubem magne claritatis descendentem de caelo in terram caliginosam die pluuiali. Et coruscantem fulgure inmenso et stetit modico spatio temporis in loco propinquo iuxta turbam illam. Et post haec exiit ad Arcem Lethglaisse[56] ubi sepultus est Patricius. Et diutius ibi moratus est nubs et illic euanuit.

Et non audebant turbae interrogare Patricium quid significaret[57] ista visio mirabilis, sed sanctam Brigitam interrogauerunt. Dixitque Brigita, 'Interrogate Patricium'. Audiens Patricius ait, 'Tu et ego equaliter scimus. Reuela eis hoc mysterium'. Dixitque Brigida, 'Nubs ista, ut puto, spiritus est patris nostri sancti Patricii, qui venit ad visitanda loca ubi corpus eius requiescet post exitum et sepelietur. Nam in loco propinquo, modico tempore, corpus eius requiescit et post hec portabitur ut sepeliatur in Arce Lethglaisse. Et ibi usque ad diem iudicii corpus eius permanebit'.

Tunc dixit Patricius ad Brigitam ut suis manibus faceret linteamen[58] et in eo postea corpus sancti Patricii involutum in loco constat.

59. Erat quidam homo nobilis et diues atque bonus in campo Mache qui habebat dolorem grauissimum et pestem et non potuit curari ab omnibus medicis. Misitque ad sanctam Brigitam ut veniret ad se. Et illa venit ad domum illius.

Illa vidisset a longe stetit et dixit, 'A quacumque parte ventus venit, ad domum istam et infert secum ille ventus maledictionem et

---

56 ledgladus L, lethglaisse P, lidgladus Z, ledchadus H
57 significat et L, significaret PZ
58 linteamen quo corpus illius post exitutem geretur optans ut cum illo linteamine ad uitam aeternam resurgeret et sic brigida fecit linteamen et in ea post modum corpus sancti patricii inuolutum est et in eo usque manet P

morbum ad virum istum'. Hoc audiens ille vir dixit, 'Nulli hominum feci malum, nec clericis lesi nec fabris'.

Tunc armentarius eius dixit, 'Audiui omnes in circuitu tuo quasi uno ore te maledicentes eo quod agricola tuos agros sepibus muniens[59] commutauit omnes vias planas et rectas in loca aspera et implana[60] et spinosa'.

Hoc audiens sancta Brigita ait, 'Haec est causa dolorum'. Tunc omnes vie conuerse sunt in vias planas et omnes viatores benedicebant illi. Et homo sanatus est Deoque et Brigitae gratias egit.

60. Quadam autem die sancta Brigida sedebat in latere oppida Mache[61] cum puellis suis. Vidit duos viros vas plenum secum portantes. Cumque appropinquassent, postulauerunt a Brigita aquam benedici et illa benedixit aquam et viros.

Euntibus autem illis, contigit ut vas illud caderet in terram super latus suum et non fractum illud vas nec aqua effusa[62] quia sancta Brigita prius benedixit. Iussit autem sanctus Patricius aquam illam seruari et aeclesiis omnibus illius regionis diuidi ut in Eucharistiam sanguinis Christi mitteretur et ut aspergerentur egri de illa aqua in sanitatem. Et ita factum est. Et laudauerunt Deum per Brigitam.

61. Misitque sancta Brigita ad sanctum Patricium ut sibi praedicaret verbum Dei dum ille cum suis discipulis et illa cum puellis suis in unum conuenirent. Patricius vero per tres dies et noctes non cessauit loqui nec sol occidit eis, sed omnes putauerunt unam esse horam.

Quidam autem ignarus rerum aliunde superuenit sancto Patricio dixit, 'Quid tanto hic tempore sedetis?' Patricius respondit, 'Quae est hora diei nunc?' Ille dixit, 'Per tres dies et noctes hic mansistis'. Dixitque Patricius, 'Per xl dies et noctes hic fuissemus nisi ad nos

59 mutens L, muniens PH
60 plana L, in plana P
61 nacem L, mache P, maceni H
62 infusa L, effusa PH

aliquis extrinsecus venisset et nullam lassitudinem vel esuriem sentiremus, diuina donante gratia'. Tunc omnes ad sua reuersi sunt.

62. Post haec venit sancta Brigita ad campum Breg. Cumque[63] habitaret sancta Brigita in alia aeclesia, venit ad eam uxor filii Conalli[64] regis ut Brigita Deum rogaret pro se quia sterilis erat. Secumque portauit fialam argenteam. Sed tamen sancta Brigita non exiit ad salutandam illam extra eclesiam sed puellam misit.

Tunc puella ad Brigitam dixit, 'Cur Dominum non rogas pro regina ut filium habeat cum sepe rogas pro uxoribus plebeorum?' Dixitque Brigita, 'Quia plebei cuncti seruiunt omnesque Patrem poscunt. Filii vero regum serpentes sunt et filii sanguinum filiique mortis, exceptis paucis electis a Deo. Sed tamen quia adiurauit nos regina, vade et dic ei semen habebit, sed tamen sanguineum et maledicta stirpis erit[65] et multis annis regnum tenebit'. Et sic fuit.[66]

63. Quadam autem die occurrit sancte Brigite quidam insanus de loco ad locum discurrens furore agitatus qui affligebat omnes ambulantes per illa loca. Dixitque ad eum sancta Brigita, 'Praedica mihi verbum Domini Iesu Christi'.

Insanus dixit, 'O sancta Brigida virgo, tua iussa implebo. Ama Deum et amabunt te omnes. Honora Deum et honorabunt te omnes. Time Deum et timebunt te omnes'.

Et cum haec dixisset, cum clamore fugit.

64. In illo die venit ad sanctam Brigitam in via ambulans Conallus filius Neil, dixitque ad eam, 'O sancta Brigita virgo, benedic me diligenter ne me occidat frater meus Corpreus[67] qui me odit'. Dixitque ei Brigita, 'Benedicam tibi. Tua familia praecedat et sequemur eos, non enim decet nos ambulare cum eis. Tu autem remane'.

63 cum L, cumque P
64 conalis L, conalli P, conallis H
65 erat L, erit PH
66 et sic impletum est P
67 corporeus L, corpreus P

Tunc illi praecesserunt. Et cum omnes per collem ascenderent, dixit una ex virginibus ad Brigitam, 'Heu Brigita, quid faciemus? Ecce Corpreus post nos venit. Et isti duo fratres nunc mutuo se iugulabunt'. Aitque Brigita, 'Non sic faciet nobis Deus noster'.

Et cum venisset Corpreus dixit, 'O Brigita sancta, benedic me, quia in his locis timeo fratrem meum Conallum'. Tunc simul duo fratres per collem transierunt nec se inuicem agnouerunt. Excecauit oculos eorum Deus ne circum[68] se agnoscerent propter sanctam Brigitam.

Et benedixit illis Brigita et osculabantur se inuicem Conallus et Corpreus, non agnoscentes se. Abiit unusquisque in uiam suam et magnificauerunt omnes nomen Dei et Brigitae in hoc miraculo.

65. Iterum alio tempore venit ad sanctam Brigitam supradictus Conallus cum suis satellitibus circumdatus sub stigmatibus malignis. Dixitque ad Brigitam, 'Tua benedictione indigemus, nam volumus in regiones longinquas ut ista vincula nostra soluumus. Est enim solutio eorum inimicos iugulare et interficere'.

Dixitque Brigita, 'Rogo Deum meum omnipotentem ut ista signa diaboli deponatis ut vultis et a nullo ledamini et nullum offendatis'. Et Christus velociter hanc voluntatem virginis impleuit. Exierunt enim in regionem Cruthniorum[69] et expugnauerunt ibi quoddam castellum et incenderunt illud, sicut visum est eis. Et putabant se multos homines interfecisse et decollasse. Et venerunt ad patriam suam cum sonitu et iubilatione[70] grandi et capitibus inimicorum.

Et cum inluxisset dies, capita et sanguinem non viderunt neque in vestimentis neque in armis nullus cruor apparuit. Dixeruntque ad inuicem cum stupore, 'Quid nobis contigit? Ubi sunt quae cernebamus?' Tunc miserunt legatos ad castellum quod succenderant

68 omit P
69 cruthiniorum L, cruthniorum P
70 iugulatione L, iubilatione PH

ut interrogarent si quid illis accidisset. Habitatores[71] illius castelli dicentes, 'Utrum aliquid nouum vobis accidit?' At illi dixerunt, 'Non nisi stipulas incensas hodie mane inuenimus distructumque castellum atque lapides grandes[72] undique conportatos reperimus. Neminem autem vidimus neque sensimus quis ita fecit'.

Legati reuertentes haec Conallo nuntiauerunt. Tunc Conallus cum suis stigmata sua diposuerunt nec contra Deum et Brigitam venerunt. Et Brigitae placuit hoc dixitque ad Conallum, 'Quia stigmata tua pro me deposuisti, in quocumque periculo me inuocaueris. Defendam te et sanus euades'.

Et hoc promissum impletum est, nam in capite anni Conallus cum exercitu multo in regiones inimicorum exiit et ibi cedem maximam fecit et cum magno triumpho reuersus est in suam patriam. Cumque fatigatus fuit in aliud castellum intrauit. Tunc socii sui dixerunt ad Conallum, 'Si in hoc loco manserimus, venient inimici nostri et interficient nos'. Dixitque Conallus, 'Lassus sum. Hinc exire non possum. Sancta Brigita promisit mihi quod me defendat in omni periculo. Credo quod illa promisit verum erit. In manus illius me commendo cum meis comitibus in hac nocte'.

Statimque in illa nocte inimici post eos venerunt. Et cum aduenissent prope ad illud castellum ubi erat Conallus, tres viros ad considerandum castellum miserunt. Et illi intrauerunt in castellum et ibi viderunt magnum populum clericorum sedentes in habitu clericali et ignem in medio eorum et libros apertos coram eis. Sic enim posuerat exercitus capita occisorum ut unusquisque caput positum ante haberet. Ideoque visi sunt viri quasi libros apertos scrutantes.

Et reuersi sunt exploratores illi talia renuntiantes. Et iterum alios tres viros sagaciores miserunt et ipsi viderunt similiter clericos cum libris apertis sicut priores viderunt. Tunc exercitus inimicorum reuersus est in suam regionem et legatos ad reportanda capita retro

71 legati interrogauerunt habitatores P
72 undes L, grandes P

miserunt qui hec Conallo nuntiarunt. Tunc Conallus gratias Deo et Brigite egit.

66. Alio tempore rogata est sancta Brigida ut exiret ad regem qui in campo Breg erat ut liberasset alium virum qui vinctus erat cum rege. Dixitque Brigita ad regem, 'Dimitte mihi virum vinctum et dabo tibi pretium pro illo'. Rex respondit, 'Si mihi dedisses totum campum Breg non dimitterem illum, sed statim in hac die iugulabitur'. Vixque obtinuit Brigita ut vita unius noctis concederetur ei.

Tunc Brigita in illa nocte in proximo loco sedit cum cognatis et amicis illius vincti eratque illa sine somno. Dixeruntque socii sui ad regem, 'Nisi in hac nocte vinctus occidatur, cras non potest occidi. Sancta Brigida eum liberauit. Statuimus[73] ergo consilium ut per vim rapiamus eum de manibus tuis et sine consilio tuo occidamus eum.[74] Et tu eris inculpabilis'.

Sed istum dolum cognouit Brigita. Ideoque in principio noctis visio apparuit vincto viditque Brigitam[75] ei stantem quae dixit illi, 'Ecce mali homines cogitant te occidere in hac nocte. Sed[76] cum traheris ab eis ad iugulandum, vocabis nomen meum sepissime. Et catena de collo tuo cum[77] ablata fuerit ut iuguleris, declinato ad nos in dexteram partem et inuenies nos statim. Exspectamus enim te'.

Evigilauit homo et statim venerunt illi et rapuerunt vinctum de manibus regis solueruntque catenam ut iugularetur. Ipse autem absolutus exiit ad Brigitam. Illi vero, ut putabant, interfecerunt virum et amputauerunt caput eius. Crastino autem die caput et cruor non apparuerunt. Tunc omnes ammirabantur stupidi. Orto autem sole, misit Brigita ad regem ut dimitteretur ei vinctus. Rex vero audiens haec penitentiam egit et dimisit vinctum liberum.

73 statui L, statuimus P
74 rapiamus de manibus tuis L, rapiamus eum de manibus tuis et sine consilio tuo occidamus eum P
75 brigita L, brigidam P
76 et L, sed P
77 omit L, cum P

67. Quadam autem die venerunt ad Brigitam quidam viri otiosi et vani habentes stigmata diabolica in capitibus suis et quaerentes aliquem iugulare. Et postulauerunt benedici a Brigita. Et illa rogauit eos vicissim ut onus graue cum operibus suis leuarent.

At illi dixerunt, 'Non possumus dimittere stigmata nostra nisi aliquis sufferat ea ne cadant in terram'. Et accepit et multum mirabatur signorum formas et signauit[78] ea signaculo crucis Christi.

Illi autem abierunt in viam quaerentes sanguinem[79] effundere. Et repererunt quemdam plebeum et iugulauerunt eum et decollauerunt. Plebeius vero ille exiit sanus ad domum suam et illi quaerebant corpus eius vel caput aut sanguinem et non inuenerunt. Dicebantque ad inuicem, 'Sanctae Brigide causa interficimus et non interficimus virum'. Et diuulgatum est hoc factum per omnem regionem. Et reliquerunt illi sua stigmata et glorificantes Deum et sanctam Brigidam magnificabant.

68. Rex quidam cum muneribus in campo Liffi ad sanctam Brigidam venit ut benediceretur ab illa. Et illa benedixit eum diligenter. Rex cum[80] reuersus est in viam suam. Nocte sequenti, cumque rex ille lassus fuit in itinere, dormiuit cum suis omnibus comitibus et custodibus.

Venitque quidam vir qui inimicus regis erat et intrauit in castellum et in domum et tenens candelam de candelabro quaesiuit regem et inuenit eum dormientem et gladium eius super ceruical iuxta se. Arripiens gladium, in cor illius tribus vicibus finxit et statim in fugam perrexit. Tunc omnes sentientes effusionem sanguinis surrexerunt et fecerunt planctum magnum putantes regem esse mortuum.

Rex vero dormiebat somno graui et postea euigilans consolatus est eos. Et post pusillum vulneratus sanus remansit dicens, 'Sanctae Brigite benedictio qua, me hodie me benedixit, illa custodiuit me'.

78 repeat et accepit multum et signauit L
79 signum L, sanguinem P
80 autem PZ

Crastino quoque die cum multis muneribus ad sanctam Brigitam rediit et illa fecit pacem inter regem et inimicum qui eum iugulauit et inter genera eorum in sempiternum, Deo donante per merita sanctae Brigide.

69. Post haec voluit sancta Brigida exire in regiones Muminensium ad peregrinandum simul cum episcopo Erco, discipulo sancti Patricii, quia gens Erci de Muminensibus erat.

Cumque intrassent in via dixit Brigita ad episcopum Ercum, 'Demonstra mihi, venerabilis pater, sub qua parte caeli gens tua consistit'. Et cum ille demonstrasset, dixit ei Brigita, 'Nunc ibi bellum geritur inter unam gentem et aliam gentem'. Dixitque Ercus, 'Credo quod dicis verum esse, nam quando ab eis huc veni, dimisi eos discordes'. Dixitque Brigita, 'Gens tua nunc in fugam vertitur'.

Tunc unus de familia Erci crepauit[81] eam dicens, 'Quomodo potes videre bellum per magna spatia terrarum?' Arguitque illum Ercus ut ne plasfemaret[82] Spiritum Sanctum. Dixitque Ercus ad Brigitam, 'Oro te, signa oculos meos et pueri istius ut videamus quae tu vides'. Tunc signauit oculos eorum et viderunt bellum oculis suis propriis. Tunc puer episcopo voce lacrimabili dixit, 'Heu, heu, domine mi, ecce modo videntibus oculis meis duo fratres mei germuni decollantur'.

70. Via postea obtata perrexerunt ad montem Ere[83] Brigita cum episcopo ibique in medio itinere fame et siti laborauerunt et nimia lassitudine fatigati. Dixitque unus puerorum, 'Magnam misericordiam faceret qui nunc nobis solacium dedisset'.

Respondit Brigida, 'Ego corde auido volo vobis solacium dare. Si ergo vultis cibo et potu satiari, expectate hic adiutorium Saluatoris. Video namque domum in qua elemosina paratur cuidam eclesie offerenda in Dei domum. Huc itaque veniet in hac hora. Ecce enim prandium in sarcinis modo est paratum'.

81 increpauit P
82 blasphemaret PZH
83 aere P, imere Z, omit HM

Adhuc illa loquente, venerunt qui elemosinam portabant. Et illi cognoscentes quod Ercus episcopus et sancta Brigita sedissent illic et fame laborassent, letati sunt valde et obtulerunt eis suam elemosinam dicentes, 'Accipite elymosinam quam vobis misit Deus. Non enim habemus meliorem eclesiam quam vos'.

Tunc illi gratias Deo egerunt comederuntque illic, sed tamen potum non habebant. Dixitque Brigita, 'Fodite in proximo terram'. Et fodientes inuenerunt fontem lucidum et iste fons manet illic usque hodie sub nomine Brigite. Tunc omnes Deum et Brigitam glorificabant.

71. Deinde venerunt ad campum Femin[84] et ibi multum sinodum et aliquantis diebus detenti sunt in sinodo. Narrauitque episcopus sinodo plurimas virtutes Brigide.

Et tunc pestilentia[85] grauis vastabat plebem omnesque rogauerunt Brigitam ut visitaret infirmos. Dixitque episcopus, 'Loca pestilentiae non ingredietur sancta Dei, sed vestros aegros ducite ad eam'. Tunc adduxerunt ad illam claudos et leprosos et daemoniacos et omnes infirmos et in nomine Iesu Christi Brigita illos omnes sanauit.

72. Post haec exiit sancta Brigita ad alium hominem qui erat secretus et solitarius et propinquus mari, haut procul ab illo loco ubi episcopus Ercus habitabat. Et mansit illic cum suis puellis annis multis, ut narratur.

Non longe autem ab eis anchorita habitabat qui facies mulierum videre vitabat, totus Deo deditus et perfectus. Postea ille anchorita voluit ire ad quendam insulam et ingrediens in viam uenit secus locum Brigidae. Comites itaque illius dixerunt, 'Eamus ad sanctam Brigitam ut nos benedicat'. Respondit anchorita, 'Scitis votum meum quod nullam feminam volo videre'.

---

84 femai L, femin PZ, femine H
85 pestilentie L, pestilentia P

Tunc surrexerunt a suis sedibus in quibus interim sederunt et obliti sunt omnia onera sua super viam et venerunt iter totius diei. Facto autem vespere sederunt in quodam hospitio et tunc recordati sunt sua onera et dicebant, 'Ideo onera nostra perdidimus, quia non declinauimus ad Brigidam ut nos benediceret'. Et pro hac culpa in hac nocte ieiunuverunt.

Mane autem facto reuersi sunt ad Brigitam et inuenerunt in domo eius onera sua. Suis namque puellis Brigita iussit dicens, 'Ite et adducite onera seruorum Dei, quae sunt in via nobis proxima, ne pereant'. Reuersis itaque illis ad Brigitam, transierunt tres dies et noctes in Dei laudibus et in praedicatione verbi Domini.

Deinde anchorita et sui exierunt in viam et exiit Brigita cum eis. Videns autem sancta Brigita onera grauia miserta est eis. Tunc in illa hora viderunt duos equos de monte descendentes ad se et inposuerunt onera sua super equos. Et cum venerunt pene usque ad finem itineris, dixit illis Brigita, 'Dimittite equos quos tenuistis'. Tunc equi fugierunt et nemo eorum nouit unde vel cuius fuerant. Brigita reuersa est ad domum suam, anachorita autem ad insulam suam exiit.

Sed laicus quidam intrauit in illam insulam cum uxore sua et filiis et filiabus. Anchorita vero deuitans videre mulierem, rogauit laicum ut exiret de insula, sed non impetrauit. Dicebat enim laicus quod haberet agrum in illa insula ex paterna hereditate.[86] Tunc misit anachorita ad Brigitam ut veniret ad se. Et illa venit et ieiunans rogauit laicum et impetrare non potuit. Crastino autem die venit ingens aquila et rapuit infantem uxoris illius laici. At illa uxor plorans et flens venit ad Brigitam. Dixitque illi Brigita, 'Noli flere quia viuit infans. Dimisit enim aquila in littore quodam super terram'. Tunc exiit uxor et sic inuenit infantem venitque ad Brigitam et penituit. Laicus vero durus permansit et inpenitens et increpens uxorem suam.

86 omit L, ex paterna hereditate PZ

Cumque esset ille laicus iuxta litus crastino die, subito venit ventus vehemens et illum trans mare in proximum portum leniter et molliter vexit. Tunc ille laicus conpunctus corde penitentiam egit et deuouit se Deo et Brigite non intraturum se[87] iterum in illam insulam nisi permisisset anchorita intrare.

73. Alio quoque die hospites religiosi venerunt ad sanctam Brigitam qui habitabant in loco iuxta litus maris. Tunc dixit Brigita cuidam viro de familia sua qui erat piscator et solebat iugulare tauros marinos, 'Vade ad mare si forte possis adferre aliquod hospitibus'.

Tunc ille exiit et adsumpsit secum hastam marinam. Statim occurrit ei taurus marinus et misit astam iacula et infixit eam in tauro. Funes enim pendebat et asta caput. Funes circa manum viri erant obnixe. Taurus vero grauiter vulneratus traxit secum virum in sua naui per mare. Et non cessauit taurus donec protinus perueniret ad Brittanie litora. Tunc funis scissus est contra saxa litoris et vir remansit in sua naui in litore. Taurus vero cum asta reuersus est in mare et venit recto itinere ad litus loci illius in quo erat sancta Brigita et ibi mortuus taurus marinus.

Vir autem ille prospera nauigatione in sua naue peruenit hora sexta et inuenit taurum mortuum cum asta in litore. Et regressus domum indicauit illis suam nauigationem. Tunc omnes gratias Deo et Brigitae egerunt.

74. Post haec venit sancta Brigita cum puellis suis in campum Clioch[88] et habitauit ibi in quodam loco. Tunc venit ad Brigitam ancilla quaedam fugiens dominam suam. Domina vero illius secuta eam volens secum revocare[89] illam. Brigita vero rogauit dominam ut dimitteret ancillam, sed domina noluit ancilla enim multas vestes texebat.

87 omit PZ
88 cliohc L, clioch PZH, chlioch M
89 reducere P, reportare Z

Tunc domina illa tenuit manum ancillae suae et traxit violenter a latere Brigidae eam ancillam et hoc Brigitae displicuit. Et cum pergissent paululum a sancta Brigita, manus dextera dominae aruit, quae tenuit manum ancillae. Videns autem domina quia non potuit mouere manum suam, fleuit et penitentiam egit et dimisit ancillam liberam Brigide. Et illa ipsa sanata est.

75. Sancta Brigita rogata est ut exiret ad quendam regem in campo Clioch ad liberandum virum qui erat in vinculis cum rege. Et exiit Brigida et intrauit in domum regis et non inuenerunt regem in domo sua, sed amici eius erant in ea, id est, vir qui nutriuit regem, cum sua uxore et filiis.

Et vidit Brigita cytharas[90] in domo et dixit illis, 'Zitharizate nobis zitharas vestras'.[91] Responderunt amici regis, 'Non sunt nunc cithariste in hac domo, sed exierunt in viam'. Tunc alicuius[92] vir qui erat cum comitibus sanctae Brigite iaculari verba illis amicis dixit,[93] 'Vosmetipsi zitharizate vobis, et benedicat sancta Brigita manus vestras ut possitis complere quod praecipit vobis,[94] et obedite voci eius'. Dixeruntque amici regis, 'Faciamus. Benedicat nos Brigita'.[95] Tunc arripiunt citharas et modulantur rudes cithariste.

Tunc rex venit ad domum suam et audiuit vocem carminis et dixit, 'Quis[96] facit hoc carmen?' Respondit ei unus, 'Nutricius tuus et nutrix tua cum filiis suis, iubente Brigita'. Intrauitque rex in domum et postulauit a Brigita benedici. Dixitque Brigita, 'Tu vicissim dimitte mihi virum vinctum'. Tunc rex gratis donauit ei vinctum. Illi vero amici regis fuerunt cithares[97] usque ad diem mortis suae et semen eorum per tempora multa regibus honorabiles valde fuerunt.

90 citharas PZ
91 citharizate nobis citharis vestris P
92 unus P, alius Z
93 iaculanti uerbo amicis dixit regis P
94 quod illa praecipit & oboedite P, quod illa precepit uobis. & obedite Z
95 faciamus ita ut nos sancta benedicat brigida P
96 quos L, quis PZ
97 citharistae PZ

76. Duo viri leprosi venerunt ad sanctam Brigidam rogantes ut salui fierent. Tunc orauit cum ieiunio sancta Brigita et benedixit eis aquam et dixit eis ut alterutrum se lauarent in aqua sancta. Et sic factum est. Et statim unus sanatur et suis vestibus lotis induitur.

Dixitque illi Brigita, 'Laua et tu socium tuum'. Ille autem videns quia mundatus est et vestimenta lauata[98] noluit tangere lepram alterius sed de sua sanitate gloriabatur. Dixit autem ei Brigita, 'Quod tu voluisti ut ille tibi faceret, te decet similiter ei facere'. Ille vero negauit et contradixit. Tunc Brigita semetipsa surrexit et mundauit leprosum et dedit ei vestimenta munda.

Ille vero qui prius sanatus est ait, 'Modo sentio scintillas ignis esse super humeros meos'. Et statim totum corpus eius lepra percussum est propter superbiam suam. Alius vero sanatus est propter suam humilitatem et gratulatus est Deo qui se per merita sanctae Brigite sanauit.

77. Quadam die sancta Brigita cum suis virginibus ambulabat campestri et vidit quendam iuuenem scolasticum currentem velociter. Ait ei Brigita, 'O iuuenis, quo tu curris tam cito?' Ille respondit dicens, 'Ad regnum Dei curro'.[99] Dixit ei Brigita, 'Utinam merear currere tecum ad regnum Dei. Ora pro me ut istud valeam'. Respondit scolasticus, 'Tu roga Deum ut cursus meus non impediatur et ego vicissim pro te rogabo ut tu et mille comites tecum vadant[100] ad regnum Dei'. Tunc sancta Brigida pro iuuenem rogauit Deum et in illis diebus ipse penitentiam egit et fuit religiosus usque ad mortem suam.

78. Duo leprosi ad Brigitam venerunt quaerentes[101] elemosinam. Illa autem nihil habens quod illis daret, unam vaccam quam habebat

98   lauate L, lauata Z
99   ad regnum dei ora pro me ut ista valeam accipere L, ad regnum dei curro dixit ei brigida ut nam merear currere tecum ad regnum dei PZ
100 uadat L, uadant P
101 quarente se L, quaerentes aelemosium illa autem nihil habens PHZ, petentes elemosynam M

dedit eis. Quorum unus gratias egit, alter vero superbus et ingratus extitit dicens, 'Nisi mihi soli detur vacca, dimidium illius non portabo'.

Tunc Brigida dixit ad humilem leprosum, 'Tu hic mecum paulisper expecta quid nobis Dominus mittet. Et ille superbus vaccam solus ferat ut ipse dicit'. Tunc exiit ille cum vacca, sed solus non potuit vaccam minare. Tandem labore fatigatus, reuersus est ad Brigitam et multis conuitiis calumniabatur sanctam Brigitam dicens, 'Quia[102] non ex corde donasti vaccam tuam, ideo solus non potui eam portare. Dura est nimium et inmitis'.

Sed sancta Brigita consolabatur eum et non potuit eum lenire. Et hoc displicuit sancte Brigite et dixit ad eum, 'Filius perditionis es. Vaccam portabis, sed tibi non proderit'.

79. Eadem die vir quidam venit ad Brigitam cum vacca in oblationem et tunc duo leprosi portauerunt duas vaccas et exierunt ad quoddam[103] flumen. Et illud flumen rapuit superbum leporum cum sua vacca in profundum et obsorbatus est neque unquam inuentus corpus eius. Humilis vero euasit cum sua vacca.

80. Post hec venit sancta Brigida a campo Clioch ad fines Laginensium ut[104] illic pauperes[105] seminis sui adiuuaret. Cumque venisset in curru suo per campum Femin,[106] inuenerunt ibi quendam virum saepientem[107] agrum. Dixitque illi auriga Brigitae, 'Concede nobis ut sancta Brigita transeat in curru per agrum tuum et postea circumdabis sepem agro tuo'. Respondit ille vir, 'Non, sed ite per circuitum agri'. Rogauerunt eum et non impetrauerunt.

Tunc dixit Brigita, 'Faciamus quod ille dixit ne aliquid contingat offensionis causa illius viri'. Tunc auriga cogebat equos transire sepem. Videns autem hoc vir ille furibundus fuste cedebat equorum

102 qui L, quia PZH
103 quondam L, quoddam P
104 et L, ut PZ
105 pauperibus P
106 femini L, femin PZ
107 sapientem L, seminantem P

nares. Equisque calcitrantibus, sancta Brigita et auriga ceciderunt de curru, sed nihil eis lesit[108] et equi steterunt in uno loco.

Tunc ait Brigita, 'Nonne dixi tibi ut hunc virum vitaremus? Vidi virum pestilentiae esse et mortis'. Tunc vir ille ceptum opus adgreditur paruipendens scelus quod fecit. Et statim ille corruit in terram et mortuus est.

81. Venit ergo sancta Brigita ad extremos fines Laginensium et intrauit in prouinciam nepotum Labrathi et ibi habitauit in quodam loco. Tunc venit ad eam quaedam femina cum filia leprosa ut sanaretur ab illa. Tunc Brigita ieiunans orauit et benedixit aquam et iussit filiam leprosam aspargi de illa aqua. Et statim mundata est a lepra sua et gratias Deo egit et Brigitae.

82. Religiosi quidam venerunt ad Brigitam et praedicauerunt verbum Dei. Post haec dixit Brigita ad cocam suam, 'Praepara prandium optimis hospitibus'. Respondit coca dicens, 'Quale prandium dabo eis?' Dixitque Brigita, 'Da eis panem et butyrum et cepas et fercula multa'. Respondit coca, 'Dabo sic, sed tu prius exi ad eclesiam. Nihil enim horum quae dicis habet coca'. Dixitque Brigita ad cocam, 'Scopa pauimentum cocine et claude eam et vade in domum tuam et ora in ea. Et ego ibo ad aeclesiam'.

Hora autem sexta vocauit Brigita cocam plausu et dixit illi, 'Adest ut reficiantur hospites. Vade ad coccinam et quodcumque inueneris in ea, da eis largiter'. Tunc illa aperiens coccinam inuenit omnes escas quas dixit Brigita et non defecerunt illae escae per septem dies et erant sufficientes tam hospitibus quam omni familiae Brigite. Et nemo nouit unde erunt iste esce aut quis eas adtulit praeter[109] Brigitam et cocam suam sanctam.

83. Alio tempore virginum chorus venit ad sanctam Brigitam habentes quaestionem et dixerunt ad eam, 'Cur in hoc loco holera equatica[110] non sunt quibus sancti homines uti consuescunt?'

108 sed lesit L, sed nihil eis lesit P
109 propter P
110 equatica L, aquatica PZH

Pro hac causa sequenti nocte sancta Brigida Dominum rogauit. Mane autem surgentes puelle viderunt fontes supra modum mensure his holeribus abundantes. Et transeuntes per longa spatia locorum et inuenerunt in illis locis nimiam multitudinem holerum istorum quae ante inuisa erant in illis locis usque rogauit Brigita et donauit ei Deus omnipotens sicut rogauit.

84. Fama sancta Brigidae crescente per multas regiones, quidam viri religiosi cum muneribus venerunt ad eam de longinquo et illa munera portabant ad eam in curribus et in equis. Sed casu venerunt in siluas condensas. Venit nox[111] super illos et ignorantes viam errauerunt in siluis neque poterant currus portare in siluis.

Tunc sancta Brigida laborem illorum cognouit et pro eis Dominum rogauit et dixit puellis suis, 'Accendite ignem et calefacite aquam hospitibus'. Nox vero illa erat tenebrosa. Tunc princeps illorum vilorum ambulantium vidit ingentem lampadem quam antecedebat eos in via usque dum peruenerunt ad domum. Tunc Brigita exiit in obuiam illis Deoque commune gratias egerunt et manserunt ibi tribus diebus Dominum laudantes.

Post haec reuersi sunt illi per eamdem viam qua venerunt illa nocte supradicta. Et viderunt loca aspera et inplana et non potuerunt currus portare nisi in humeris suis et equi in manibus et maximo labore euaserunt quia nemo nouit peritorum esse viam in illis locis. Sed Christus in nocte supradicta illa loca fecit plana et lucida propter sancta Brigidam rogantem.

85. Simili modo quidam episcopus nomine Broon, quem supra diximus, venit cum muneribus ad sanctam Brigitam et cum curribus et equis et cum multo populo comitantium. Venerunt et ipsi in siluas densas et errabant ignorantes viam sicut praescripsimus accidisse. Tunc[112] nox hiemalis cecidit super eos.

111 *omit* L, nox PZ
112 tam L, tunc PZ

Sancta autem Brigita hoc sciens dixitque puellis suis, 'Oremus Dominum pro hospitibus, quia laborant venientes ad nos, ut misereatur Deus labores eorum. Mira valde dicturus sim'.

Tunc hospites illi in media via protinus viderunt locum Brigitae, sicut putabant,[113] videruntque letam Brigidam cum suis puellis venire in occursum eorum cum pace. Quae subito duxit eos in magnam domum curribus equisque detractis, abluit pedes eorum abundantiaque ciborum refecit eos. Stratis quoque lectis hospites collocauit et omnia quae necessaria sunt hospitibus fecit eis Brigida cum puellis suis, sicut senserunt.

Mane autem facto, dixit Brigita puellis suis, 'Properemus in obuiam hospitibus errantibus iuxta nos, qui hac nocte in silua manserunt'. Tunc festinauerunt et inuenerunt hospites in silua sedentes et cum ingenti laetitia deduxerunt eos ad domum suam et compleuerunt omnia iura hospitii quae ostensa sunt hospitibus in nocte et simul gratias Deo egerunt.

86. Sanctus episcopus Broon reuersus est ad suam regionem et portauit secum chrismal a sancta Brigita. Ille autem habitabat iuxta mare.

Quadam vero die episcopus laborabat in litore maris et unus puer secum et positum est istud chrismal super saxum in litore et venit mare ad plenitudinem suam. Tunc puer recordatus est chrismal et fleuit. Dixitque episcopus, 'Noli flere. Credo enim quod chrismal sanctae Brigitae non peribit'. Et completum est. Chrismal enim siccum super saxum fuit et non mutatum est fluctibus maris. Et decrescens mare, illud inuenerunt sicut positum est.

87. Post haec venit sancta Brigida ad domum patris sui Dubthachi volens post longa tempore visitare parentes. Et pater eius gauisus est valde in aduentu ipsius et rogauit eam ut in domo sua mansisset in illa nocte et illa mansit.

---

113 portabant LZ

In hac autem nocte venit angelus et suscitauit Brigidam et iterum veniens suscitauit eam. Tertia autem vice paulo grauius excitauit eam dicens, 'Surge cita patrem tuum et suam familiam et tuas puellas, nam hostes adpropinquant et voluntes occidere patrem tuum cum sua familia. Sed propter te non vult Deus hoc. Exite cito nunc, statim exite, nam domus ista nunc conburetur'.

Et cum omnes exirent, hostes statim venerunt et succenderunt domum. Tunc pater ipsius dixit, 'O sancta Brigita, tua benedictio nos custodiuit in hac nocte a morte praesenti'. Dixitque illi Brigita, 'Non solum in hac nocte, sed usque ad senectutem sanguis non effundetur in habitaculo vestro'. Usque quod huc per multa tempora completum est. Nam cum quidam voluisset percutere gladio quandam virginem, riguit manus eius quam extenderat et non potuit manum retrahi donec illam virginem dimisit.

Crastino autem die dixit una puellarum suarum ad sanctam Brigitam, 'Utrum angelus adiuuaret te semper sicut fecit in nocte transacta'. Ait autem Brigita, 'Non ista nocte tantum, sed per omnem aetatem meam auxilium eius habeo in omnibus. Nam cottidie laetitiam praestat mihi, dum per ipsum caelestium sonos et spirituales cantus organorum cottidie audio. Sanctorum quoque missas qui Domino procul in terra caelebrant, quasi prope essent per ipsum cottidie audire possum. Et meas orationes nocte ac die offert Deo et in praesentia et in absentia semper audit me. Quod duobus exemplis nunc tibi demonstrabo.

'Quodam autem tempore rogauit me mulier quaedam leprosa et infirma ut ei aquam differrem et in ceteris necessariis sibi misericorditer ministrarem. Vas itaque cum aqua benedixi et dedi ei dicens, "Pone illud inter te et parietem ne aliquis praeter te tangat illud donec reuertar". Angelus vero benedixit illam aquam in absentia mea et conuersa est in omnem saporem quemcumque leprosa volebat. Nam quando mel concupiscebat, saporem mellis habebat. Similiter quando vinum siue cereuisam vel lac aut alias liquores eadem aqua in sapores eorum per mulieris infirmae voluntate vicissim vertebatur.

'Item cum ergo parua puella essem, feci altare lapideum ludo puellari venitque angelus Domini et perforauit lapidem in quattuor angulis et subposuit quattuor pedes ligneos.

'Hec duo de angelo meo, O puella, tibi monstraui ut Dominum nostrum glorificeris'.

88. Eodem tempore sanctam Brigidam pater suus rogauit ut iret ad regem Laginensium ut gladium quem ille rex patri suo pro tempore donauerat in perpetuum daret. Exiit itaque sancta Brigita ad regem in campo Liffi.

Cumque illa sedisset ad portam ciuitatis ipsius, venit ad eam unus seruorum regis dicens, 'Si me obsolueris ex iugo regis istius, seruus tuus ero in perpetuum cum omnibus meis et ego et cognati mei Christiani erimus'. Dixit illi Brigida, 'Peto pro te'.

Tunc Brigita vocata est ad regem. Dixitque ei rex, 'O Brigita, quid vis a me?' Ait ei illa, 'Ut detur gladius tuus patri meo ut unum de seruis tuis mihi dimittas'. Dixit rex, 'Quid mihi dabis pro his duabus magnis petitionibus?' Ait Brigida, 'Si vis, vitam aeternam dabo tibi et semen tuum reges erunt per secula'. Dixit rex, 'Vitam quam non video non quaero. De filiis qui post me erunt, non percuro. Alia vero da mihi duo: ut longeuus sim in praesenti vita quam diligo et in omni loco et bello victor existam. Iugem enim[114] pugnam habemus contra nepotes Neil'. Dixit illi Brigita, 'Hec duo tibi dabuntur: longe vita et victoria in omni bello'.

Nec multo post haec exiit ille cum paucis hominibus in campum Breg. Cumque videret multitudinem hostium, dixit ad suos, 'Vocate Brigitam in auxilium ut sancta impleat sua promissa'. Et clamauerunt ad caelum. Tunc statim rex vidit sanctam Brigitam praeire ante se in pugnam cum baculo suo in manu dextera et[115] columna ignis ardebat de capite eius usque ad caelum. Tunc hostes in fugam versi sunt. Rex vero cum sua familia gratias Deo et Brigite egerunt.

114 ingemen in L, lugem enim P, lugemen Z
115 *omit* L, et columna ignis ardebat de capite eius usque ad caelum PHZ

Post haec ille rex xxx bella gessit et vicit omnia, nouemque certamina in Britannia prospere egit, et a multis regibus merces ei dabatur ut cum ipsis pugnasset quia ille erat inuictus.

89. Factum est autem post mortem illius regis,[116] venerunt nepotes Neil ut delerent Laginensis. Tunc Laginenses consilium bonum invenerunt[117] dicentes, 'Ponamus corpus mortuum regis nostri inter nos in curru et pugnemus circa cadauer eius contra hostes'. Et ita fecerunt. Tunc nepotes Neil in fugam versi sunt. Donum enim diuinum per sanctam Brigitam in rege mansit et sic post mortem illius regis.

90. Alio quoque die quidam vir sanctus venit ad domum in qua sola Brigita orabat et inuenit eam stantem et manus in oratione tendentem in caelum. Et nihil aliud videbat nec audiebat. Eadem hora clamor magnus habitatorum loci illius insonuit, nam ad vaccas vituli hora ipsa inruerunt. Sed haec sancta non audiuit in mentis excessu Deo intenta.

Tunc vir ille reliquid eam in hac hora ne conturbaret orationem eius. Alia vero hora reuersus est ad eam et dixit ei, 'O sancta Dei, cur non curristi ad clamorem plebis?' Ait illa, 'Clamorem autem istum non audiui'. Dixit ei vir ille, 'Quid aliud audisti?' Respondit Brigita, 'In urbe Roma iuxta reliquias sancti Petri et Pauli audiui missas et nimis desidero ut ad me ordo missae istius et uniuerse regule deferatur'.

Tunc misit Brigida viros sapientes ad Romam et detulerunt inde missas et regulam. Item post aliquantulum tempus dixit Brigita ad illos viros, 'Ego sentio quod quaedam commutata sunt in Roma missa postquam venistis ab ea. Exite iterum'. At illi exierunt et detulerunt ut inuenerunt.

91. Quadam autem die pluuiali venit Brigita ad domum suam. Et cum cessaret pluuia, radius solis venit in domum per parietem. Et

116 reges L
117 inuerunt L, inuenerunt Z

posuit Brigita vestimentum suum super illum radium, putans quod funis esset. Tunc alius praedicauit verbum Dei in domo illa et Brigita intendebat verbum Dei et usque ad vesperam et ad magnam partem noctis, inebriata est mens eius verbo Dei et oblita est praesentia.[118] Radius vero ille super quem posuit Brigita vestimentum suum madidum[119] post occasum solis usque ad dimidium noctis permansit.

Tunc unus eorum qui erant in domo illa dixit ad Brigitam, 'Tolle vestimentum de radio solis quia radius iste usque ad mane non deficiet donec tollas vestimentum tuum de eo'. Tunc Brigita cito surrexit et deposuit vestem de radio dicens, 'Putabam quod funis esset non radiis'. Alii quoque eadem nocte venerunt ad campum Liffi et dixerunt se vidisse radium istum inlustrantem campum donec pervenerunt ad sanctam Brigidam media nocte. Tunc omnes Deo gratias egerunt et laudauerunt sanctam Brigidam.

92. Post haec exiit sancta Brigita ut peregrinaret in regionibus Connahctorum[120] cum duobus episopis quibus[121] simul secum comitantibus et habitauerunt ibi in campo Aii.[122]

Quadam ergo die accessit ad altare ut Eucharistiam sumeret de manu episcopi et calicem desuper intuens vidit in eo formae prodigium, id est, umbram hirci vidit in calice. Unus quippe de pueris episcopi calicem tenebat. Tunc Brigida noluit bibere ex hoc calice. Dixitque ei episcopus, 'Cur non bibis ex hoc calice?' Brigita manifestauit ei quod in calice vidit.

Tunc episcopus puero dixit, 'Quid fecisti? Da gloriam Deo'. Puer autem ille confessus est se fecisse furtum cum caprario et unum hircorum suorum occidisse et ex parte comedisse carnes eius. Dixitque ei episcopus, 'Penitentiam age et funde lacrimas cum fletu'. Et iussis obediuit puer et penitentiam egit. Iterum vocata Brigita,

118 sentia L, absentia P, praesentia ZH
119 in radium L, madidum PZ
120 connahctorum L, connachctorum P, cognathorum Z
121 quibus L, quibusdam PZ
122 au L, aii P

venit ad calicem et illa vice nihil vidit hirci illius in calice. Lacrimae enim illius culpam soluerunt.

93. In alio tempore in eadem regione quaedam decrepita anus[123] infirmabatur ad mortem veneruntque ad eam omnes virgines loci illius ut vigilarent et orarent cum ea in domo. Et sancta Brigita venit cum eis.

Tunc quaedam ex virginibus ait, 'Tollantur vestimenta de ea ne sub ipsis mortua fiat et ne laboremus lauantes ea in tempore frigoris et niuis'. Hoc sancta Brigita prohibuit dicens, 'Paruo tempore vobiscum erit. Facite illi misericordiam ad paruam horam'.

Egrediente vero anima illius vetule de corpore, visa sunt vestimenta extra domum et nemo vidit quis ea foras portauit. Caritas enim cordis Brigitae utrumque voluit, ut infirma illa vetula non nudaretur vestibus in magno frigore et ut virgines non laborarent in magna frigore. Utrosque ergo liberauit a vi frigoris. Tunc omnes Deum et sanctam Brigitam laudauerunt.

94. Cum sancta Brigida ibidem habitaret in quadam aeclesia, stagnum aquae frequentabat. Quadam autem nocte in qua erat nix et glacies, omnibus dormientibus, venit Brigita ad stagnum cum quadam puella. Et erat Brigita in illa nocte in stagno orans et flens. Et quod semel fecit in illa nocte, hoc semper omnibus noctibus voluit facere et in consuetudinem vertere. Sed Christi misericordia hoc fieri diutius non passa est.

Alia namque nocte stagnum illud inuenerunt siccum sine aqua nisi arena sicca tantum. Prima vero hora diei venientes ad stagnum, plenum inuenerunt aquam ut semper fiebat. Similiter secunda nocte iterum aruit stagnum, diebus vero plenum aque fiebat. Ita ut Deus manifestaret omnibus magnam virtutem virginis Brigite.

95. Orta est magna quaestio apud Laginenses de absentia sancte Brigite miseruntque nuntios ad eam in regiones Connachtorum ut ad suam gentem rediret. Tunc Brigida venit cum eis.

123 decrepitanus L, decrepita anus P

Cumque venerunt ad flumen Sinne, inuenerunt ibi iuxta Uadam Luain[124] duas plebes sedentes ex utraque ripa, id est, nepotes Neil et Conachtorum gentes. Tunc puellae sanctae Brigidae postulauerunt ab omnibus ut trans flumen portarentur in ratibus eorum et non impetrauerunt. Quidam vero pessimus homo dixit ad illas, 'Date mihi unum vestrorum sagorum et in mea naue trans flumen portabo vos'. Dixeruntque puellae, 'Non, sed nos nunc ibimus in flumen et benedictio sanctae Brigitae custodiet nos'.

Eadem hora dixit Brigita puellis suis, 'Signate istud flumen in nomine Iesu Christi ut micius et humilius efficiatur nobis'. Tunc sancta Brigita, duobus populis adstantibus, ut diximus, cum puellis suis intrauit in flumen et usque ad genua virginum non peruenit alueus ingentis fluminis quod etiam fortissimi viri sine naue non poterant transire. Omnes itaque Deum et sanctam Brigitam laudauerunt.[125]

Et priusquam sancta Brigita intraret flumen cum puellis suis, ingressi sunt in paruam ratem alii clerici, qui se confitebantur in inperitia nauigandi, et illi dixerunt ad Brigitam, 'Poterit ratis ista portare unam puellarum tuarum nobiscum'. Tunc Brigita iussit uni puellarum ut ante se praeiret cum eis trans flumen. Dixitque puella, 'Benedic me diligenter, timeo enim a te separari in flumine'. Dixit ei Brigida, 'Vade in pace, Dominus custodiat te'. Tunc nauigauerunt et in medio fluminis mersa est nauis sub aquam cunctis videntibus. Tunc puella in periculo posita clamauit nomine sanctae Brigite in auxilium. Et benedixit eam Brigita et orauit pro illa sedente super aquam. Et portauit eam aqua in sua sede usque ad portum cum siccis vestimentis. Tunc omnes confessi sunt mirabilem Deum omnipotentem in sancta Brigita virgine.

96. Dum ergo sancta Brigida venisset ad patriam suam, cum magno honore et gaudio totius plebis suscepta est.

124 nadam luit in L, uadam luain P, nadum lua ZH
125 sanctam lauderunt brigidam P

Quodam autem tempore erat panis inopia cum virginibus Brigitae in loco in quo habitabant. Tunc quidam qui habitabat in orientali plaga campo Liffi venit ad Brigitam, vir bonus et largus, et dixit ad eam, 'Veniant mecum puellae tuae ut adferant tibi aliquantos modios'.

Tunc exierunt cum eo et reversi sunt puelle cum oneribus ab illius hominis. Cumque venissent ad amnem Liffi, inuenerunt illum plenum ultra ripas abundantia maxima aquarum et non potuerant amnem transire undis tumescentibus. Tunc virgines quid agerent stupida mente ignorabant. Tunc prostrauerunt in terram iuxta ripam fluminis et inuocabant una voce sanctam Brigitam in auxilium. Continuoque simul ab eo loco in quo erant in alteram ripam fluminis translate sunt cum oneribus suis. Et quomodo aut qualiter translate sunt ignorabant.

Tunc venerunt puelle ad sanctam Brigitam et narrauerunt ei miraculum quod factum est ipsis. Et ipsa praecepit eis ut nemini dicerent hoc miraculum. Sed tamen celari non potuit.

97. Sancta Brigita habebat quandam alumnam nomine Darlugdacha, quae alio die non bene custodiens oculos suos vidit alium virum et concupiuit eum et ipse similiter amauit eam. Tunc ergo haec virgo in quadam nocte conduxit illum virum. Et illa nocte erat ipsa virgo in uno lectulo cum sancta Brigita.

Cum autem paulisper dormiret sancta Brigida, surrexit virgo. Et cum processisset de lectulo inruit in eam mira perturbatio cogitationum et magnum enarrabileque certamen habebat in corde, id est, inter timorem et amorem. Timebat enim Deum et Brigitam et vehementissimo igne amoris viri urebatur. Orauit ergo Dominum ut adiuuaret eam in magna angustia. Tunc inueniens a Deo bonum consilium, impleuit duos ficones suos carbonibus ignis et intinxit duos pedes suos in eos. Et sic factum est ut ignis ignem extingueret et dolor dolorem vinceret. Atque retro in suum lectulum reuersa est.

Haec autem omnia sensit Brigita, sed tamen tacuit ut puella paulisper temperaretur et ut probaretur. Crastino vero die puella confessa est suum peccatum. Dixitque ei Brigita, 'Quam viriliter dimicasti in hac nocte. Et pedes tuos in praesenti combussisti ignis fornicationis iterum in praesenti et ignis Gehenne in futuro te non comburet'.

Tunc sanauit Brigita pedes eius combustos ita ut nec vestigium quidem combustionis appareret in eis, quasi ignis non tetigisset eos.

98. Alio die messores sancta Brigida in messem suam vocauit. Et dies pluuialis erat illa et per totam illam prouinciam pluuiis abundanter effusis, sua messes sola arida sine pluuiarum inpedimento perstetit. Et cum omnes messores illius regionis illa die pluviali prohibiti essent, sui messores, sine ulla umbra caliginis, tota die ab ortu solis usque ad occasum per Dei potentiam opus exercebant incessabiliter cum serenitate.

99. Alio itidem die tribus aduenientibus episcopis et cum ea hospitantibus, dum non haberet sancta Brigita unde eos cibaret, adiuta multiplici Dei virtute, vaccam unam contra consuetudinem in una die tribus vicibus mulsit. Et quod solet de optimis tribus vaccis exprimi, mirabiliter de una sua vacca expressit.

Hanc autem vaccam sciens alius puer rogauit sanctam Brigidam ut donaret ei eam. Et postquam portauit similis omnibus vaccis effecta est. Et quaecumque vacca fiebat apud Brigitam, talis fiebat qualis supradicta fuit.

100. Alio quoque die venit quaedam mulier ad sanctam Brigitam dicens, 'Quid faciam de puero meo? Quia pater eius vult occidere eum nam pene obortiuus[126] est. A natiuitate enim cecus est, tabulatam faciem habens.'

Tunc Brigita mulieri miserta est iussit faciem pueri in aqua propinqua lauare. Et statim sanus factus est puer, qui vocabatur cretanus. Quem adfirmant usque ad mortem dolorem oculorum non habuisse sed sanos oculos semper habebat.

126 abortiuus ZH

101. Alio itidem die quidam puer alacer venit ad sanctam Brigitam sciens illam misericordem esse in pauperis. Causa ludi et iaculari verbo[127] aliorum, postulauit ab ea berbicem de grege in forma pauperis veniens. Et illa donauit ei berbicem. Et ille iterum venit vii vicibus et vii berbices in nomine Domini postulans per astutiam in forma pauperis veniens, ab ea ut voluit portauit. Sed vespere facto dinumeratoque grege, certus numerus inuentum est. Item additis berbicibus vii gregi in nocte qua causa erat ludi nihil superfluum mane inuentum est.

102. Mirabili quoque eventu ad Brigitam leprosi ceruisam postulantes, cum non haberet illam videns aquam ad belneum portatum[128] virtute fidei benedicens, in optimam ceruisam conuertit et abundanter sitientibus exhausit.

103. Alio autem die sancta Brigita per potentissimum fortitudinem fidei aliquam feminam post votum integritatis lapsam et habentem pregnantem ac tumescentem vuluum benedixit. Et decrescens in vulva conceptus sine partu et dolore, eam sanam ad penitentiam restituit. Illa sanata est et gratias Deo egit.

104. Quadam autem die cum quidam ad Brigitam veniret salem petens, sicut ceteri pauperes profulsis necessitatibus venire solebant. Sancta Brigita autem salem non habens in promptu, salem factum de lapide quem benedixit in manum poscentis largita est. Et sic ab ea salem portans. domum cum gaudio rediit.

105. Alio die sancta Brigita suam mentem de terrestribus ad celam elevans, partem grandem larde cum cane dimisit. Et cum pars illa esset incessita non alicubi sed in loco canis solebat esse, mense transacto, intacta et integra reperta est. Non enim canis ausus est comedere depositum beate Brigite virginis. Sed custos patiens et idoneus larde contra suum solitum morem diuina virtute refrenatus indomitus extitit.

127 uerba L, uerbo Z
128 bellania porta L, balneam portatum Z

106. Alio quoque die cum alius pauper cibo indigens eam rogaret, illa ad alium virum qui carnes coxerat perrexit ut pauperi aliquid quaereret. Sed ille stultissimus famulus qui carnes coxerat partem carnis nondum coctam in sinum ipsius proiecit, candide[129] vestis scilicet. Sic et illa pauperi tribuit non suffocato colore candide vestis sed manente in sua naturale colore.

107. Alio itidem die cum aper feris[130] singularis[131] et siluestris territus et fugitiuus esset, ad gregem porcorum Brigite felicissime cursu praecipiti peruenit. Quem ipsa inter sues suas[132] cernens, benedixit. Deinde inpauidus ac familiaris permansit in grege ipsius porcorum quia et bruta animalia et bestiae sermonibus et voluntati eius resistere non poterant. Domita et subiecta placida seruitute sibi ut volebat famulabantur.

108. Alio autem tempore sancta Brigita fortissimum virum, nomine Lugidus,[133] nimia essione sanauit, quem asserunt in uno prandio manducare bouem et porcum cum pane sufficiente. Quanto enim hominibus virtute supereminebat, tanto essione praecellebat. Hunc ergo similem ominibus hominibus essione fecit, nulla virtute priuata.

109. In alia nocte fuit carus laicus cum sua uxore in hospitalio apud sanctam Brigitam. Et ille rogauit Brigitam ut signaret vuluam uxoris ut filium habuisset. At Brigita fecit. Et statim in illa nocte ipse cum uxore dormiuit. Inde natus est Etchenus sanctus praecipuus.

In illa autem nocte lunulum[134] argenteum mulieris illius laici quaedam ancilla furata est. Et in crastino die multis hominibus exeuntibus post eam, lunulam[135] illam in amnem maximum eiecit.

---

129 cottidie L
130 feris L
131 strangulans L, singularis ZH
132 sus L
133 lugidus L, lugidum Z
134 anulum L, lunulam Z

Et unus piscis statim mire magnitudinis eam devorauit. Piscatores quoque in illa hora eum piscem in retibus suis tenuerunt et ilico ad sanctam Brigitam illum piscem in oblationem portauerunt. At ille piscis incissus suam lunulam laici uxori Brigita reddidit. Tunc ille cum sua uxore pregnante gratias Deo agentes et Brigita in suam viam perrexit.

110. Alio tempore venit sancta Brigita ad aliam virginem religiosam. Illa autem non habens aliud nisi unum vitulum, parauit caenam sanctae Brigite de vitulo unius vacce sue et super lignale sue assauit eum. Audiens sciensque hoc, sancta Brigida mane renouiuit haec omnia, id est, vitulus ad matrem suam mane peruenit et lignatile renouata mane inuenta sunt sic ut antea fuerunt.

111. Alio tempore sancta Brigita missalia vestimenta Conlaidi episcopi pauperibus dedit, quia aliud quod daret eis non haberet. Et statim in hora sacrificii, Conlaidus suum vestimentum quaesiuit dicens: 'Corpus Christi et sanguinem non immolabo sine meis vestimentis'. Tunc Brigita orante, similia vestimenta Deus praeparauit et omnes videntes glorificabant Deum.

112. Alio quoque tempore sancta Brigida vestimenta in scrinio super mare misit ut deuenirent per longissimum spatium maris ad Senanum episcopum in alia insula marina habitantem. Et ille Spiritu Sancto reuelante fratribus dixit, 'Ite quantotius ad mare et quicquid inueneritis hunc vobiscum deducite'. Illi autem exeuntes inuenerunt scrinium cum vestimento ut diximus. Senanus vero videns gratias egit Deo et Brigite, quod enim homines ire non possunt sine maximo labore scrinium solum Deo gubernante perrexit.

113. Alio quoque die sancta Brigita proiecit massam argenti in flumen ut veniret per illud ad aliam virginem, nomine Hinna, quae paullo antea respuit eam massam portare. Et sic postea, Deo deducente, accepit.

135 lunulum L

114. Quadam die alius reus perductus ad iugulandum ab alio rege. In hora autem iugulationis eius, sancta Brigida orans, argentum a Deo in sinum accepit et regi pro eo reddedit. Et ille reus de morte liberatus est.

115. Die quoque alio sancta Brigita unam tunicam duobus pauperibus diuisit. Utrumque dimidiam tonice in illa hora plena esse tonica effecta est a Deo.

116. In alio die sancta cum digitis suis petram durissimam perforauit, necessitatem enim maximam habuit quam nunc tacemus causa brevitatis.

117. Sancta Brigita filiam alicuius principis liberauit, nam cum illa virginitatem suam Deo servire voluisset et pater eius coegisset eam in coniugem, nocte nuptiarum praeparatis epulis, relinquens parentes ad sanctam Brigidam confugit. Quod mane pater secutus est, sed viso equitatu[136] eius procul a Brigita signo crucis inpresso terre omnes fixi sunt. Et mox ut penitentiam egit cum suis solutus est. Et sic filia liberata est a carnali sponso et colligata est Christo, sicut in suo corde vouit.

118. Alius rex superbus respuit principem quem sancta Brigita volebat in alia ciuitate fieri. Et rex statim de curru cecidit et capite conliso ad terram mortuus est.

119. Alio tempore cogente pauperitate et inminentibus hospitibus urticas[137] mutauit in butyrum et cortices arborum in lardam pinguissimam et dulcissimam.

120. Sancta Brigita promisit alio mago obuiare ei in hora mortis eius, qui sibi heretlitatem dedit. Quod ita factum est. Cum enim ille iacuisset in lectulo exspectans mortem, dixit familiae suae, 'Disponite cito omnia necessaria quae sunt, nam video sanctam

136 equitatui L
137 urticam LH

Brigidam in veste candida cum multis mihi obuiare'. Et sic baptizatus est et Deo credens defunctus est.

121. Quodam tempore sancta Brigida et sancta Ita, cognomento Daritha,[138] conloquentes invicem de Christo simul non senserunt noctem. Ubi enim sol iustitie Christus praesens fuit, nihil tenebrosum relinquebat.

Tunc dixit Ita ad Brigitam, 'Benedic mihi oculos meos ut valeam mundum videre sicut desidero'. Oculis enim illa orbata erat. Tunc benedixit Brigita oculos eius et statim aperti sunt. Sancta Ita vero dixit, 'Iterum reclude oculos meos. Quanto enim quis mundo absentius fuerit, tanto praesentius Deo erit'. Et sic iterum clusit Brigita oculos eius sicut illo rogabat.

122. Alia nocte sancta Brigita sola cum Deo adiutorio inmobile lignum mire magnitudinis transmutauit, quod lignum prius plurimi homines mouere non poterunt. Angelus autem Dei cum Brigita usque ad locum quae volebat duxerunt.

123. Quodam quoque tempore quaedam mulier cum filia muta ad eclesiam sancte Brigite perrexit et vocauit ad se aliam virginem, Darluchoacham[139] nomine, dicens ei, 'Dispone mihi ut filia mea alumna sanetur'.

Tunc illa portauit filiam ante conspectum Brigidae dicens ei, 'Hac filia ad te venit. Loquere ei'. Tunc Brigita eam interrogauit dicens, 'Utrum vis virgo permanere an ad nuptias copulari'. Nesciebat quod illa muta esset. Statimque illa respondit dicens, 'Quodcumque mihi dixeris, ego volo facere'. Et sic postea usque ad mortem suum in eloquentior omnibus fuit.

124. Alio die vidit Brigita anates[140] natantes in aqua et interdum per aera volantes eos ad se venire arcessiuit.[141] Quae obedientes

138 darihta L, dario H, daria M
139 darluchoacham L
140 amantes L, nantes nantantes H
141 arcessint L

vocibus eius sine ulla formidine multitudinis ad eam volitabant, quas manu tergens et amplectens per aliquantum temporis redire permisit.

125. Quadam die cum alius rusticus nulla suffultus scientia per regis palacium videret vulpem. Putans quod non mansueta et familiaris esset et quod variis artibus docta regi et suis comitibus spectaculum praestaret, et ignoraret, vidente multitudine, occidit eam. Tunc alligatus est et ad regem perductus fuisset, illum occidi nisi vulpis similis in omnibus calliditatibus restituta esset, et uxorem et filios et omnia quae habuit in seruitutem redigi.

Cum sancta Brigita rem gestam didicisset, misericordia permota et pietate, currum sibi iungi praecipiens et pro misero precibus ad Dominum profusis, perrexit in viam quae ducit ad palacium regis. Nec mora Dominus eius misertus est unumque de suis vulpibus feris ad eam transmisit. Et in currum ad eam intrauit et subueste Brigitae se constituens, sobrie in curru cum ea sedebat.

Cum ergo Brigita ad regem peruenisset, coepit praedicare ei ut miser inprovidus soluetur. Sed rex noluit, obsistans quod non dimitturus esset illum nisi vulpem similem in omnibus calliditatibus restituisset. Tunc ipsa vulpem suum protulit in medium et omnes mores alterius agens, variis lusit artibus coram omnibus. Tunc rex placatus dimisit reum liberum abire.

Cum vero sancta Brigita remearet ad domum suam, soluto vere praedicto, ipsa vulpes dolosa in turbus callide mouens ad loca deserta et ad suum antrum refugit. Et equitibus canisque persequentibus, incolomis euasit. Et omnes videntes admirati sunt virtutem Dei per Brigitam.

126. Cum aliquando alius vir ad sanctam Brigitam venisset offerens ei sues pingues, dixit ad eam, 'Veniant a te comites mecum ad meam villam ut tibi sues producunt'. Quae villa longo intervalla oberat ab eclesiae sanctae Brigide, spatio itineris trium vel quattuor dierum.

Tunc Brigita dimisit comites cum illo, sed transacto unius diei itinere in monte cofinali, quas in longinquo opinabatur esse, obuias ad se venire et a lupis ad se directis coactasque per viam contemplati sunt. Et cum ille cuius essent intellexisset proprius sues a lupis a campo Fee minatus de siluis maximis pro reuerentia beate Brigite et a lupis ille[142] miratus est valde, dans gloriam Deo.

Et sic altero die hi qui missi fuerant a Brigita cum suibus factum mirabile narrantes domum reuersi sunt et omnes gratias Deo egerunt.

127. Alio die inuenit Brigita mel in pauimento domus sue quod antea ibi non fuit. Sed in illa hora Deus sanctae Brigitae commendauit quia illa quadam necessitate cogente mel a Domino suo postulauit et sic inuenit.

128. Alio die sancta Brigita per virtutem Dei aliud flumen de suo loco in alterum locum mutauit. Et prima vestigia illius usque in hodiernum diem hominibus apparent.

129. Cum autem sanctae Brigitae exitus de hoc saeculo adpropinquasset, voluit alumna sua Darlugdacha secum egredere de hac vita. Respondit ei Brigita dicens, 'Successor mea eris in uno anno. Et in die obitus mei ut una nobis solemnitas sit morieris'. Et sic factum est.

Sancta vero Brigita migrauit de hac luce post victoriam inter choros patriarcharum et prophetarum atque apostolorum et martyrum omniumque sanctorum ac virginum et inter angelorum et archangelorum agmina ad coronas eternuas regni celestis, ad Hierusalem celestiem, ad regnum sine fine ubi praemia aeterna praestantur per Dominum nostrum Iesum Christum filium tuum.[143]

142 ille suas L
143 omit filium tuum HM

FURTHER READING

Bieler, Ludwig, 'Saint Bridget' in R. Hayes (ed.), *Manuscript sources for the history of Irish civilisation* (Boston, 1965), pp 331–4.

Bitel, Lisa, *Land of women: tales of sex and gender from early Ireland* (Ithaca, 1996).

— 'Body of a saint, story of a goddess: origins of the Brigidine tradition', *Textual Practice* 16:2 (2002), 209–28.

— 'Ekphrasis at Kildare: the imaginative architecture of a seventh-century hagiographer', *Speculum* 79 (2004), 605–27.

— *Landscape with two saints: how Genovedfa of Paris and Brigit of Kildare built Christianity in barbarian Europe* (Oxford, 2009).

Bray, Dorothy, 'The image of St Brigit in the early Irish church', *Études celtiques* 24 (1987), 209–15.

— 'Saint Brigid and the fire from heaven', *Études celtiques* 29 (1992), 105–13.

— 'Ireland's other apostle: Cogitosus' St Brigit', *Cambrian Medieval Celtic Studies* 59 (2010), 55–70.

— 'The *Vita Prima* of St Brigit: a preliminary analysis of its composition', *CSANA Yearbook* 8/9 (2011), 1–15.

Collins, Tracy, *Female monasticism in medieval Ireland: an archaeology* (Cork, 2021).

Connolly, Seán, '*Vita Prima Sanctae Brigitae*: a critical edition with introduction, commentary and indices' (PhD, NUI, 1970).

— 'The authorship and manuscript tradition of *Vita I Sanctae Brigitae*', *Manuscripta* 16 (1972), 67–82.

— '*Vita Prima Sanctae Brigitae*: background and historical value', *The Journal of the Royal Society of Antiquaries of Ireland* 119 (1989), 5–49.

Connolly, Seán, and Picard, J.-M., 'Cogitosus' *Life of St Brigit*: content and value', *The Journal of the Royal Society of Antiquaries of Ireland* 117 (1987), 5–27.

Dawson, Elizabeth, 'Brigit and Patrick in *Vita Prima Sanctae Brigitae*: veneration and justification', *Peritia* 28 (2017), 35–50.

Esposito, Mario, 'On the earliest Latin Life of St Brigid of Kildare', *PRIA C*, 30:11 (1912/13), 307–26.

— 'Cogitosus', *Hermathena* 20 (1926), 251–7.

— 'On the early Latin Lives of St Brigid of Kildare', *Hermathena* 24 (1935), 120–65.

Freeman, Philip, *The world of Saint Patrick* (Oxford, 2014).

— 'The Life of Saint Brigid by Cogitosus', *Proceedings of the Harvard Celtic Colloquium* 39 (2019), 109–33.

Harrington, Christina, *Women in a Christian church: Ireland 450–1150* (Oxford, 2002).

Howlett, David, '*Vita I Sanctae Brigitae*', *Peritia* 12 (1998), 1–23.

Kissane, Noel, *Saint Brigid of Kildare: life, legend and cult* (Dublin, 2017).

Maney, Laurance, 'The date and provenance of *Vita Prima Sanctae Brigitae*', *Proceedings of the Harvard Celtic Colloquium* 23 (2003), 200–18.

McCarthy, Daniel, 'Topographic characteristics of the *Vita Prima* and *Vita Cogitosi Sanctae Brigitae*', *Studia Celtica* 35 (2001), 245–70.

McCone, Kim, 'Brigit in the seventh century: a saint with three Lives?', *Peritia* 1 (1982), 107–45.

— *Pagan past and Christian present in early Irish literature* (Kildare, 1990).

McKenna, Catherine, 'Between two worlds: Saint Brigit and pre-Christian religion in the *Vita Prima*' in Joseph F. Nagy (ed.), *Identifying the Celtic: CSANA Yearbook* 2, (Dublin, 2002), 66–74.

Ó Brian, Felim, 'Brigantana', *Zeitschrift für celtische philologie* 36 (1978), 112–37.

Ó hAodha, Donncha, 'The early Lives of Saint Brigit', *Journal of the County Kildare Archaeological Society* 15 (1974/75), 397–405.

— *Bethu Brigte* (Dublin, 1978).

Oxenham, Helen, *Perceptions of femininity in early Irish society* (Rochester, 2016).

Sharpe, Richard, '*Vitae S Brigitae*: the oldest texts', *Peritia* 1 (1982), 81–106.

INDEX